HATSHEPSUT'S TEMPLE AT DEIR EL BAHARI

HATSHEPSUT'S TEMPLE AT DEIR EL BAHARI

FREDERICK MONDERSON

SUMON PUBLISHERS

FREDERICK MONDERSON

SuMon Publishers
PO Box 160586
Brooklyn, New York 11216

sumonpublishers.com@sumonpublishers.com
blackfolksbooks.com@blackfolksbooks.com
fredsegypt.com@fredsegypt.com
blackegyptbooks.com@blackegyptbooks.com

Copyright Frederick Monderson/SuMon Publishers, 2011, 2nd Edition, 2021. All Rights Reserved. No part of this book may be reproduced, stored in a retrieval system, or transmitted by any means without the written permission of the author or publisher.

ISBN – 978-1-61023-016-2
LCCN - 2010918492

In the Tribute to Professor George Simmonds, "Unsung Hero," Dr. Fred Monderson sat at the feet of his heroes, Brother X, Michael Carter, Dr. Leonard Jeffries, Elombe Brathe, Dr. Lewis, Prof. George Simmonds, Dr. ben-Jochannan, Sister Camille Yarbrough, among others.

HATSHEPSUT'S TEMPLE AT DEIR EL BAHARI

One of few *Ma'at-Ka-Ra* names of Queen Hatshepsut in Cartouche or Shennu that have escaped the destructive hands of her enemies.

FREDERICK MONDERSON

Dr. Frederick Monderson displays some of his books offered for sale at Brooklyn Book Fair, September 2010 at Boro Hall.

ABOUT THE AUTHOR

Frederick Monderson is a retired college professor and school teacher who taught African History in the City University of New York and American History and Government in the New York public schools. He has written nearly 900 articles in the New York Black Press, *Daily Challenge*, *Afro Times* and *New American* newspapers. In this venture, Monderson lends his expertise as a historian, Egyptologist, journalist and author of several books including *Michael Jackson: The Last Dance, 50 on Point, Black Nationalism: Alive and Well, Barack Obama: Ready, Fit to Lead, Barack Obama: Master of Washington, D.C., Sonny Carson: The Final Triumph*, and on ancient Egypt *Seven Letters to Mike Tyson on Egyptian Temples, 10 Poems Praising Great Blacks for Mike Tyson, Intrigue Through Time, Temple of Karnak: The Majestic Architecture of Ancient Kemet, Where are the Kamite Kings?, Abydos and Osiris, Temple of Luxor, Medinet Habu: Mortuary Temple of Rameses III, The Quintessential Book on Ancient Egypt: "Holy Land"* (A Novel on Egypt), *Research Essays on Ancient Egypt, The Majesty of Egyptian Gods and Temples* (a book of Egyptian Poems), *Egypt Essays on Ancient Kemet, The Ramesseum: Mortuary Temple of Rameses II, The Colonnade: Then and Now, Reflections on Ancient Kemet, Grassroots View of Ancient Egypt*

HATSHEPSUT'S TEMPLE AT DEIR EL BAHARI

and Glory of the Ancestors: *19 Letters to O.J. Simpson on Ancient African History*. A student of the esteemed Dr. Yosef ben-Jochannan, Dr. Monderson conducts tours to Egypt.

For Tour information, please contact Orleane Brooks-Williams at Nostrand Travel, 730 Nostrand Avenue, Brooklyn, New York 11216. Phone Number 718-756-5300.

THE MAIN SANCTUARY OF AMON-RA – THE BARK HALL

"An axial sanctuary to Amun-re - accessible from peristyle courtyard through a granite portal and limestone vestibule was composed of interconnected rooms: the Bark Hall (1), the Statue Room (2), two transversal chapels dedicated to the gods of the Great Theban Ennead (3-4), and finally the Innermost Sanctuary (5). Usually, the complex was accessible only to the king and to the priests responsible for performing the rituals. First room roofed with corbel vault was one of the largest and most impressive all over the temple. During the Feast of the Valley (beginning of summer) hosted the sacred bark of Amun coming yearly from Karnak to Deir el-Bahari. Here the final episodes of religious liturgy were celebrated and the god spent the night. In the Third Intermediate Period the Upper Terrace including sanctuary was used as necropolis, however soon afterwards (7-6th Century BC) the sanctuary hosted again the sacred bark of Amun. In the 2nd century BC, the innermost chamber was refurbished and the sanctuary was devoted to the cult of two deified personages: Imhotep and Amenhotep son of Hapu. Both of them were also associated with wisdom and medicine. In front of the entrance to the complex a small portico (6) was added. At the end of the 6th Century AD former sanctuary, then used as a sanatorium under the Ptolemies, became part of a Coptic monastery of St. Phoibammon."

FREDERICK MONDERSON

Deir el Bahari – Image of the Entrance to the Main Sanctuary of Amun-Re – The Bark Hall before excavation and restoration.

Deir el Bahari - Wearing the White Crown, Thutmose III kneels to make a two-handed presentation to enthroned Amon Re. Notice the young king's partial Cartouches or Shennus above.

HATSHEPSUT'S TEMPLE AT DEIR EL BAHARI

Deir el-Bahari - Erik Monderson assumes the regally correct stance of right above left arm on the Upper Terrace before one of several surviving statues of Queen Hatshepsut.

FREDERICK MONDERSON

Deir el Bahari - Men-Khepper-Ra cartouche of Thutmose III whose name was first prominent in this temple before the Queen took over completely.

FOREWORD

Following the debate on the ethnicity of the ancient Egyptians, just as with Hatshepsut, every shred of evidence pointing to her and their blackness or their being Negro, African, is generally discounted by European critics and their American counterparts. Whether it's the "Negro Bones of Hen Nekht" (First Dynasty); the Middle Kingdom pharaohs are thought to be "Hyksos rulers;" Aahmes Nefertari and her grandson Thutmose I generally pictured black, yet, not really accepted as such; and King Tutankhamon's statues stated as "only painted black for the funeral ceremony;" questions the proponents of such ridiculous positions. That Osiris is the "Great Black" is given as such because he is god of the dead, of a dark underworld. Naturally, we query Min's black statues in Ashmolean Museum recluse! What of Mentuhotep's "black flesh" statue? Is it true, Amon's blackness has to do with the night sky? How about Ptah not being a bald-headed pygmy (Twa), but an elf? Could Maherpra really be "Negroid but not Negro?" And so, we could go on indefinitely! Are such seeming popular yet indefensible positions as

HATSHEPSUT'S TEMPLE AT DEIR EL BAHARI

articulated, be considered misleading, or are these people ignorant of the facts? While some may say no one knows the ethnicity of Hatshepsut, she is assumed to be Caucasian! Yet, careful examination of her survived features in the interior of the Red Chapel clearly shows an African woman. Notwithstanding, beyond speculative linguistic evidence that linked ancient Egyptians and South-West Asia, now generally discredited since ancient Egyptian has been proved an African language, why are such theories still valid? Is Wortham's "Caucasian theory" based on Granville's dissection of a mummy in 1825 valid today? How about the Louvre scribe with "blue eyes," are they inlaid?

The question becomes simply this, beyond all the hoopla, "Why are so many Western, European and American scholars, ordinary people, misled on the issue of the ethnicity of the ancient Egyptians?" Is it because of the preponderance of Egyptian artifacts in Europe and America acquired in the 19th and 20th centuries that such makes the ancient Egyptian culture Caucasian? Naturally, such is a ridiculous contention. However, despite what is said, Cheikh Anta Diop's critique is as credible as ever! That is, the "African Origin of Civilization: Myth or Reality!"

Deir el Bahari - View of the Temple from the "Bird's Eye View" on the mountain; with the Lower, Middle and Upper Colonnades visible; and the Upper Court with the Portico to the Sanctuary against the mountain as a backdrop. Further on is the Temple of Mentuhotep II of the Middle Kingdom whose temple was transitional from the Old to the New Kingdom.

FREDERICK MONDERSON

Table of Contents

	Foreword	8
	Preface	13
1.	Poem: Senmut's Praise of Queen Hatshepsut.	19
2.	Poem to the Temple of Deir el Bahari	30
3.	The Temple of Deir el Bahari: An Overview.	38
4.	"An Important Archaeological Discovery In Egypt."	43
5.	The Temple of Deir el Bahari: An Introduction	53
6.	Queen Hatshepsut – Maat-Ka-Ra of the 18th Dynasty	77
7.	Senmut – Architect of Queen Hatshepsut.	128
8.	"Important Archaeological Discoveries In Egypt."	161
9.	"The Discovery at Thebes, Egypt."	185
10.	"The Archaeological Discovery at Thebes."	190
11.	"A Waif from Dayr el	

HATSHEPSUT'S TEMPLE AT DEIR EL BAHARI

	Baharee."	194
12.	"The Excavations at Deir el Bahari."	196
13.	"The Excavation of the Temple of Queen Hatshepsut At Deir el Bahari."	205
14.	"The Temple of Queen Hatasu at Deir el Bahari."	212
15.	"The Royal Mummies of Deir el Bahari."	219
16.	"The Dahr el Bahari Mummies."	227
17.	"The Deir el Bahari Mummies."	229
18.	"The Exploration of Der el Bahari."	231
19.	"The Excavations at Deir el Bahari."	238
20.	"The Excavations at Deir el Bahari."	245
21.	The Deir el Bahari Exhibition.	249
22.	Fine Art. Egypt Exploration	

FREDERICK MONDERSON

	Fund: "Deir el Bahari."	253
23.	Deir el Bahari: A Final Reflection or Postscript.	262
24.	New Revelations About Egypt's Queen Hatshepsut	277
25.	Conclusions	283
26.	Additional Reference	288
27.	After Word	296

Deir el Bahari 1. View of the temple's three levels, two ramps, stations of the guards and "black-top" leading to this magnificent piece of classical Egyptian architecture.

"The central motive of the decoration on both side walls (southern and northern) of the Bark Hall was nearly identification depiction of the processional bark of Amun in which the god's statue was brought to Deir el-Bahari during the Feast of the Valley. The god who normally dwelt in Karnak left his lonely shrine crossed the Nile and navigated the temples of deified kings as the festival was also to the memory of deceased pharaohs. A drawing of the relief from the southern wall shows portable bark of Amun resting in the middle of the Bark Hall at Deir el-Bahari temple. The processional statue of the god was hidden in a richly decorated cabin set up on the deck. On the deck there are also the figures of goddesses Hathor and Ma'at and various types of statues. The original, much smaller,

HATSHEPSUT'S TEMPLE AT DEIR EL BAHARI

image of bark from the times of Hatshepsut destroyed by Akhenaton has first been restored by Tutankhamon, and then enlarged by Horemheb."

Deir el Bahari – Another view of the full face or front elevation of the temple showing the three levels clearly.

PREFACE

Hatshepsut's Temple at Deir el Bahari is a truly unique temple that blends hand in glove with the magnificent cliffs of the surrounding mountain that forms the backdrop of this spiritually inspired piece of mortuary architecture. A fine example of classical early eighteenth dynasty building techniques that has retained its attractiveness, it remains one of the most amazing tourist attractions in all of Egypt, despite its almost 3500-year age and been exposed to the vicissitudes of the elements and man, it still exudes its ancient seemingly magical, even mystical spirituality. Thus, this temple's magnetic attraction makes its artistry a sought after and spellbinding sight to behold for the untold numbers of visitors who come to imbibe in its mystique, and appreciate, more important, to photograph its architectural beauty.

More than any other monument in Egypt, this wonderful piece of early New Kingdom architecture must be considered in several phases. From its initial conception to current day methods of preservation and accessibility for the many who flock to Thebes particularly to view this archaic splendor, its white limestone reflecting against the golden background of the mountain, is visible from a distance, even from across the Nile river. Significantly, however, new attention was recently paid the temple in the overall upgrade of all monuments in Egypt, but more particularly as the Queen's mummy was identified and thus her name and persona further rescued from oblivion by the scientific sleuthing of a team spearheaded by Zaki Hawass. Special consideration was thus lavished on this work of art to further enhance its attractiveness while also contributing to the overall security of the monument and its visitors. The Sanctuary is today accessible and so too the restored Chapel of Ra-Horakhty with its in situ 9-step altar on the north side of the Upper Court.

From the time Senmut, the architect, conceived the project mirroring the nearby Mentuhotep structure, under Hatshepsut's instruction aided by Amun's guidance; the laying of the foundation stone and the attendant ceremony as at the founding of a new temple of which archaeologists have unearthed evidence here; to the completion of the task, this work was one of great inspiration. As such, in Senmut the man, we see a tremendously creative individual who, not only completed this masterpiece but also perceived, perhaps because of political dynamics, that this beautiful temple would later be attacked and so taking attendant precautionary measures, we see revealed a great visionary. That being the case, a three story building when one was the ancient norm; and, considering when the author of the "Seven Wonders of the World" made that famous pronouncement, one has to wonder at the selection method. Then again, such a work of beauty may not have been known to the "selection committee!" Even more so, of those great architectural accomplishments, how interesting only the Great Pyramids have survived of the known "Wonders" and Hatshepsut's Temple at Deir el Bahari, not given ancient recognition of its artistic, architectural and metaphysical beauty, one has to wonder was it because the builder was a woman that it was not numbered among those spectacular architectural feats.

HATSHEPSUT'S TEMPLE AT DEIR EL BAHARI

Without a doubt the temple, Deir el Bahari, whose Arabic name means "Convent of the North" was physically attacked by a rival party who defaced the Queen's images, destroyed her statues, and even changed inscriptions to confuse posterity as to its founder. It suffered under the Amarna Revolution when Aton's adherents attacked Amon's images. Repairs done by Rameses I's 19th Dynasty artists did not do the temple justice. It suffered under Christians and was later occupied by Coptic monks. These religious adherents did damages to the temple, intentionally or unintentionally, by removing stones in their redecoration of the structure for their occupation and this occupancy itself also took a toll on the holy place. Nevertheless, with time the building fell into oblivion, yet got casual mention by visitors from the Middle Ages onwards and into early modern times. However, in the upsurge of interest in Egypt following Champollion's decipherment of Hieroglyphics and the destructive era of the "Rape of the Nile," men of true science and conscience endeavored to place the discipline of Egyptian archaeology on a more systematic footing thereby provide for preservation and safety of the monuments. Among those giants were Auguste Mariette, Flinders Petrie, Amelia Edwards and Edouard Naville, the Swiss Egyptologist. Dr. Naville got a concession for the Egypt Exploration Fund and began clearance of Deir el Bahari in the mid-1890s. He was successfully able, on a limited budget, to free the temple from all encumbrances revealing the splendid creation that has so amazed scholars and laymen from time immemorial. His efforts were aided by H.R. Hall who reported Dr. Naville's thoughts and findings as the excavation unfolded.

Recognizing that the amphitheater with its imposing cliffs would dwarf any structure designed for height, the queen and her architect chose instead width, lines and distance to layout her masterpiece. In this respect, Michael Haag, in *Cairo, Luxor, Aswan* (Guilford, Connecticut: The Globe Pequot Press (1993) 2000) has stated, "If it is true that circumstances dictated this decision, or suggested that the alternative was now pointless, it is no less true that the new form was seized upon with conviction and executed with genius. The terraces of Hatshepsut's temple emphasize the stratification of the cliff behind and the line between rock and sky. At the same time, the bold rhythm of the pillared colonnades, vertical shafts of light-reflecting stone framing and contrasting with the shadowed ambulatories, reflect the dark gashes of gullies and fissures in the cliff face itself. Even the peak seems brought into the conception: a pyramid offered by nature. The temple mediates between the wildness of the mountain and the cultivation of the valley. The power and contradiction of the landscape is gripped and tamed with a confidence and elegance that is breathtaking, and then played throughout the structure so that as you walk round the temple you feel it, never too much, but to a measure that insists on the spiritual nature of man."

Regarding this spiritual nature, divinely inspired and the exploitation of the natural surroundings, Henri Stirling's *Architecture of the World: Egypt* (Germany: Benedikt Taschen, ND: 88) offers the following description about architecture and the environment in Egypt. He writes: "The extraordinary harmony between the overall forms of Egyptian monuments and the landscape has frequently been stressed. The temples, with their simple shapes, extended proportions and clean, horizontal rooflines, echo the calm progression and dominating horizontal lines of the cliffs, particularly those to the west of the Nile, which border the valley south of Cairo." However, questioning whether these factors apply to Deir el Bahari he writes further:

"In a wide amphitheater formed by the cliffs whose abrupt drop is broken by fallen rocks, lies a superimposition of three long colonnades of polished stone, the uppermost of which has to a large extent crumbled away. These colonnades echo the drop of the cliff; the ramps and what is left of the terraces are related to the fallen rocks."

"Many commentators have taken this exceptional harmony to be proof of a completely aesthetic outlook regarding the siting and form of monuments. Others, however, have realized the danger of crediting the ancients with a preoccupation more in line with the spirit of the twentieth century than with the more primitive

HATSHEPSUT'S TEMPLE AT DEIR EL BAHARI

mentality of pre-Greek antiquity, and consider this harmony between nature and architecture to be unconscious. The architect Ricke was probably the first to accentuate correctly the relationship between the cosmic symbol and this adaptation to the landscape. The exterior of the temple at Deir el Bahari only echoes the dominant lines of the Egyptian landscape in a very general, disuse manner; like most of the other temples it freely integrates itself with a predetermined part of the landscape. The beauty of its severe lines increases the divine nature of the section of the mountain formed by the temple. Thus, this harmony with the setting, which we regard as an aesthetic achievement, has been consciously worked out, but for theological rather than architectural reasons."

Deir el Bahari 1a. An "old Photograph" viewed from the mountain showing the Second Court inward, with visitors but none on the Upper Terrace and Court, at that time undergoing repairs by a Polish Team of archaeologists. The temple of Mentuhotep is further on.

Deir el Bahari 1b. View of the twin temples from the southwest. While some features are similar others are different.

FREDERICK MONDERSON

"In a ceremony that took place in the Bark Hall Hatshepsut accompanied by Thutmosis III and princess Neferure presented offerings to the bark mounted at the prow and the stern with ram-headed aegis of the god Amun. On the south wall queen's depiction (left) was replaced with the effigy of Thutmosis III. The uraeus attached to the front protects the king against evil. The nemes headdress of Thutmosis III is striped blue imitating lapis lazuli. The deceased members of the royal family represented behind Thutmosis I, Ahmes and princess Neferubiti profited from the liturgy performed for Amun-Re (above right)."

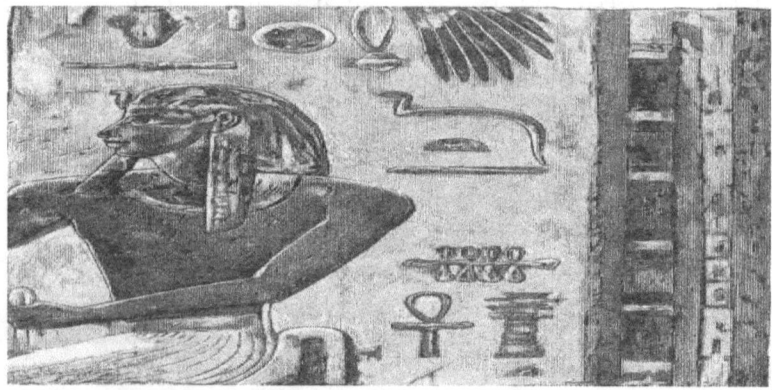

Illustration 1. Queen Hatshepsut in male costume.

Deir el Bahari – Queen Hatshepsut kneels to present two ointment jars before a "Table of Offerings" in the Sanctuary.

HATSHEPSUT'S TEMPLE AT DEIR EL BAHARI

1. SENMUT'S PRAISE OF QUEEN HATSHEPSUT
A Poem
By
Frederick Monderson

Daughter of Amon-Ra, Hatshepsut, Maat-Ka-Ra, Her Majesty, Living forever, Queen of Egypt, Land under your Dominion. From the First Occurrence, Amon Lord of Thebes prophesied your birth and promised you great power, Royal Dignity. The Great God decreed you exercise kingship. Consecrated to the Gods and purified with spiritual force Water, in an epoch of ancient African glory, you challenged male supremacy to rule a kingdom and preside over a period of prosperity, art and architectural majesty, with Life, Stability and Health. Your accomplishments testify to boldness, God-like appearance, and beauty undergirding Black assertiveness. Given Life like Ra, Forever, Great in Oblations, O, Majesty of your Father, the Maker of human beings, Maker of Truth, he blessed you with the throne of Egypt/Kemet and vision to execute divinely inspired durable projects.

Beloved, Khnemet-Amon Hatshepsut, with 12 Kas, you are more beautiful than anything. Boastful of kinship with Black-skinned Goddess Nefertari, your reign unfolded through divine inspiration and guidance. Made Wise by Amon's Excellent Spirit, Mistress of Offering, charm, beauty and intellectual daring symbolizes your integrity, and political astuteness, Horus Forever. O, Daughter, mother, lover, builder, innovator, administrator and divinity, you celebrate many jubilees, for the heavens cover and the earth encircles you. Your father is Amen, fair of face, Beneficent Bull of the Company of Nine Gods. His names are many, countless, how many cannot be known for he is wide of stride. His form shines forth at the First Occasion and as the Great Cackler, he came into being at the First Occasion.

FREDERICK MONDERSON

Mighty in Strength, Obelisks and architectural marvels attest your desire to praise African gods who advanced your nation and inspired your people by their sincere blackness and clarity in Judgment. Today your image inspires many Black women to be the 'First Queen.' Glorious in Magic, how boastful is your Black ancestral heritage in Aahotep, Hetepheres, Tetisheri and particularly Aahmes-Nefertari; later Queen Tiy and Nefertari, great king's wife, follow your lead. All the gods, Amon, Mut, Khonsu, Hathor, Thoth, Khnum, Anubis, Selkhet, Kheseti, and Atum came to endow you with years. Divine Consort, *His Majesty Herself*, your Beauty the Spirits of Heliopolis fashioned. Your father Amon is the Lord of All, the first to exist. He came into existence in the beginning and none knew his mysterious nature. He shattered his egg himself.

Deir el Bahari 1c. Beyond the First Security Gate, visitors coming and going, with essential features of the Temple visible.

Daughter of Ra, on the Throne of Electrum, you inspired architects to defy the ordinary and erect monuments praising your paternal and spiritual fathers. These noble gestures show love for great Africans, Thutmose and Amon, man and god. Such thinking reflects the great legacy you bestow on progeny who look on your history to gain strength, similarly meet challenges and raise notable African families. Support and inspire Black men, O Black Queen, as they

HATSHEPSUT'S TEMPLE AT DEIR EL BAHARI

chart the waters of new Horizons, into a new Millennium. Beautiful Lady, your father, President of his palace, is born early every day at dawn to rise in the Eastern Horizon; his day's work done, he sets in the Western Horizon as Lord of Truth. All knees spread at his presence, all cattle frolic before his entrance, Prefect seizing his opportunity and none repel him.

O Great Lady, Pure in Food Offerings, your Lineage is Divine. Amon visited your mother who slept in beauty of her palace. The God's Fragrance woke her, and in amorous encounter he conceived your divine birth. Meskhenet, goddess of births directed the midwives. She extended her arms before his majesty. Freshness in Years, Amon extended the Symbol of Life and Khnum Fashioned your Limbs. A brilliant mind envisioned such a concept, later to inspire Amenhotep III. His temple at Luxor and yours at Deir el Bahari, beautifully and graphically depict the experience of power manifesting in spirit through divine intervention, to create dynamics of social, artistic, philosophical and theological change furthering man's growth.

Golden Horus, Favorite of the Two Goddesses, Embraced by Amon, you are Powerful in the Two Lands. Horus Mighty in Ka your divine form flourishes as your father, more eminent over nature than any God to whom praise is given in the Great House. It is his soul, men say, which is in heaven. His image is not spread out in Books. He is too mysterious that his glory should be revealed. Too great so that men should ask questions concerning him. Too powerful that he should be known.

Brilliant Emanation of Amon, your mortuary temple at Deir el Bahari with chapels to Anubis and Hathor erected by a humble architect Senmut, was inspired by love of a prototype and a beautiful Black lady. Love for God, incisive use of power and sincerity and integrity in Ma'at, echo creation in process, Life and Satisfaction. O Maiden, Beautiful and Blooming, Fresh in Years, you celebrate a glorious Past, which comes from Amon to appear on the throne of Horus, like Ra. You mirror the efforts of the Lord of Graciousness who is greatly beloved. He comes and sustains mankind. He sets in motion everything that is made. He works in the celestial waters making to be the pleasantness of the light. He is Ra who is worshiped in the Apts.

Deir el Bahari – Nubians in the temple carrying flowers, standards and weapons. Notice the last individual carrying the "Curved sword."

Deir el Bahari – The starry filled sky of the "Vault of Heaven" as envisioned in the Anubis Shrine.

HATSHEPSUT'S TEMPLE AT DEIR EL BAHARI

Deir el Bahari - One of the few images of the Queen to escape the defacement of her enemies. Wearing the White Crown, necklace and beard and kilt with apron and uraei, she offers five objects. Above, her name has been erased from the cartouches.

FREDERICK MONDERSON

Deir el Bahari 2a. Hatshepsut in Karnak. The image of Queen Hatshepsut; wearing the Red Crown and dancing before Amon, as the ithyphallic Min; is erased as shown in room beside the Sanctuary at Karnak temple. Though time has begun to erode the color of Min he is still shown to be colored black. Notice how neat and systematic the erasure is indicating this was a deliberate and painstaking attempt to remove the Queen from historical recognition.

"Partly preserved exposed triangular structure from the times of Hatshepsut above the rock sanctuary of Amun-Re prior to the restoration works undertaken by the Polish-Egyptian Mission. (left) Huge blocks of limestone leading against each other reduced the pressure of the rock-massive and successfully protected the corbelled ceiling of the Bark Hall. (right, before the final stage of the conservation work.)

HATSHEPSUT'S TEMPLE AT DEIR EL BAHARI

Deir el Bahari 2b. Hatshepsut in Karnak. Another systematic erasure of Queen Hatshepsut and her Ka as she presents a sumptuous feast to Amon, in plumes and holding scepter and ankh, wearing a beard and necklace. Notice his tail behind.

Beautiful Black Pharaoh, King of Upper and Lower Kemet/Egypt, some see you as the first great woman of history. Your efforts portray great courage, wisdom and fortitude. With daring you styled yourself Chief Spouse of Amon, the Mighty One, the Lord of East and West, the Good Goddess, the Pious Lady, the Beautiful Falcon in her Risings, while your servants proclaim *Her Majesty Himself*. You rule like the one of many crowns in the house of the Ben-Ben stone. He is the God Ani, the Lord of the Ninth-day Festival. The Festival of the Sixth-day and the *Tenat* Festival are kept for him. He is king, Life, Health, and Strength to Him, as to you, Beautiful Maiden. Your father is fair of face when he comes from God's land.

FREDERICK MONDERSON

Mistress of the Two Lands, Divine in Diadems, the Electrum of Kings, you Give All Life and Satisfaction. All Stability, All Joy of Heart, Favorite of the Two Goddesses, you advocate your Truth. The inspiration Amon provided to secure Obelisks at Karnak mirrors your efforts linking Deir el Bahari to Valley of Kings by tunnel manifesting theological and metaphysical creativity. All while the Heavens Labor for you respecting the Greatness of the Fame of your Father Amon. He is a Beautiful Governor crowned with the White Crown, Lord of Light, Creator of Splendor. He gives his hand to him that loves him. His Flame destroys his enemies. He hears the cry of him that is oppressed and gracious to him that appeals to him. He delivers the timid man from the man of violence and regards the poor man, considering his misery, all traits you espouse.

Deir el Bahari 2c. Hatshepsut in Karnak. The Gods Horus (left) and Thoth (right) baptize the queen with Ankhs for long life. Notice the systematic nature of the erasure.

HATSHEPSUT'S TEMPLE AT DEIR EL BAHARI

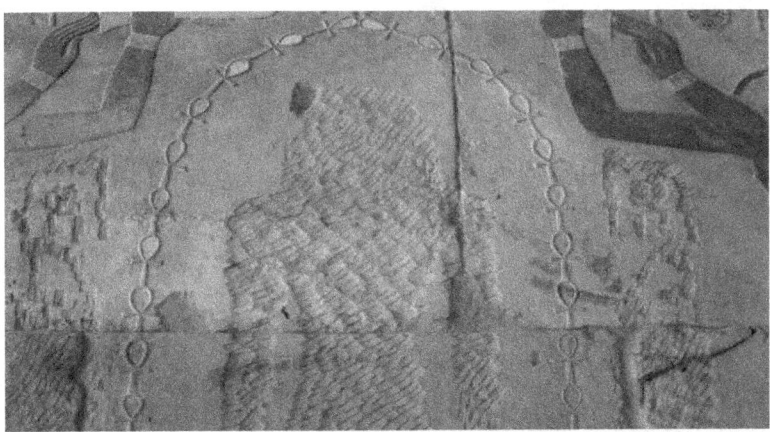

Deir el Bahari 2d. Hatshepsut in Karnak. Close-up of the gods Horus (left) and Thoth (right) baptizing Hatshepsut with Ankhs. Notice the erasures and even accompanying graphics are similarly treated.

Deir el Bahari 2e. Hatshepsut in Karnak. Left side view of the previous image showing Horus baptizing Hatshepsut with Ankhs for long life.

FREDERICK MONDERSON

Deir el Bahari 2f. Hatshepsut in Karnak. Close-up of Thoth baptizing Hatshepsut. Notice accompanying inscriptions are also erased.

Direct passage from mortuary temple to tomb utilizes a brilliant Old Kingdom concept. Architectural nicety in proportion, lines linking columns in the shadow of cliffs with powerful reflection at evening time convey the awe, Majesty and Reverence, Intellect, Wisdom and Hidden-ness of the Inexplicable Nature of Amon, worshiped here, Everlasting. Amon gave you Lands which the Sun Encompasses and Established Your Great Name like the Heavens that you may be Given Life. Only he is Amon and Ra and Ptah, together three. Father of Fathers, and Mother of Mothers, he is the Bull for the Four Maidens. The Mighty One of mysterious birth, he created his own beauty. The Divine God who came into being of himself, of mysterious forms and gleaming shape, he is the wondrous God with many forms.

HATSHEPSUT'S TEMPLE AT DEIR EL BAHARI

0 Revered Amon, Lord of Heaven, Lord of Earth, Lord of the Two Lands, Looking at your Sanctuary in *Ipit Isut*, with great praise, radiates light in inspirational fortitude. We beseech thee, continue to inspire Africa's sons and daughters and support their efforts to help humanity. All this, in the same manner Maat-Ka-Ra, Hatshepsut, worshipped you in splendor and in true religion, with art, joy and festivity. Bestow that divine inspiration, wisdom, fortitude and humility that Black men and women will continue your task of saving the children, blessing the elders and invigorating our leaders to prevail in sincerity, fortitude, truth and love.

Deir el Bahari 3. From the mountain, view of the First and Second Courts with First and Second Ramps. Clearly, the Second Security Checkpoint stands before the barrier to the First Court. Columns and pillars of the Chapel of Hathor are visible below.

FREDERICK MONDERSON

Illustration 2. Photograph of the Temple's reconstruction. (Restoration from a design by M. Brune.) Notice how the columns extend in the truly Northern Colonnade.

2. Poem to the Temple of Deir el Bahari
By
Frederick Monderson

Deir-el-Bahari, you are Hatshepsut's monument to her father, the Good God, Amon Lord of Heaven. Queen Makere, the ever-living, a brilliant emanation of Amon-Ra ruled the Black and Red Land. One who had no enemy in any land, she boasted 'my fame is among the sand-dwellers, my boundary extends from Punt to Asia and the Asiatics are in my grasp.' She ruled like the Son of Isis and strong like the Son of Nut, so her temple shall be unto eternity like an imperishable star. He, father Ra himself is united with his body and he is the great one who is in Heliopolis, the begetter of the Primordial Gods. One falls down dead on the spot for terror if his mysterious unknowable name is pronounced. No god can address him by it, he with the soul, whose name is hidden, for that he is a mystery.

HATSHEPSUT'S TEMPLE AT DEIR EL BAHARI

Amon, Lord of the Two Lands established her name on the *Ished* Tree in life, stability, and satisfaction. Makere, living forever, female Horus, Shining in Thebes, is Beloved of Amon, Lord of Diadems. Boasting, 'my father Amon favors me and my nostrils are filled with satisfying life,' she is truthful in sight of her father. Fresh in years, beautiful to look upon, with fidelity of heart, Hatshepsut is Amon's Daughter of Truth who glorifies him. Divine of Diadems who abounds in deeds and Favorite of the Two Goddesses, she boasted, the Royal Lord 'Ra, the electrum of Kings, loves me.' Beloved, she built him a temple called *Tcheser Tcheseru*, 'Most Splendid,' because the gods fawn at his feet when they know his majesty their lord. All gods make the boast in him, in order to magnify themselves with his beauty, for his is so divine.

Deir el Bahari – The refreshment stand that provides relief from the hot temperatures.

Deir el Bahari – Life, health., dominion stability, etc.

FREDERICK MONDERSON

Illustration 3. Bust of Queen Hatshepsut wearing headdress and beard.

An inscription depicts Senmut, the Steward of Amon, architect and confidante of your Queen, giving praise to Hathor for the sake of life, prosperity and health of Makere. Monuments abound justifying Hatshepsut's right to rule. Praising Amon, Maker of all beings, Lord of the Terrestrial Thrones, Senmut erected two obelisks of her four at Karnak, whose rays flood the two lands and the Sun rises between them as he dawns in the Horizon of Heaven. This master of Mankind, King, Lord of All Gods, created the fruit trees, made the green herbs and sustains the cattle as he traverses the firmament in Peace, King of Upper and Lower Egypt/Kemet.

HATSHEPSUT'S TEMPLE AT DEIR EL BAHARI

An Avenue of Sphinxes then Causeway led from the Nile into your august temple oriented southeast by northwest. Imitating Mentuhotep's earlier structure, Deir el-Bahari, you are built in three terraces when one-story structures were the norm. Trees and lions greet the visitor at your precinct entrance pylon, where flagstaffs flew the colors. Pillars alternate with columns in your First Court and the central ramp's South Colonnade. In your Lower Terrace, the Mythological and Obelisk Colonnades recount significant milestones in the queen's reign, in praise of the god of the beginning, firm of horns and fair of face, who is Crowned in the House of Fire.

Deir el Bahari 3a. The Amphitheater covered in a blanket of debris up to the cliffs that challenged early archaeologists who cleared the site and revealed the majestic structure of this classical New Kingdom temple.

Deir el Bahari – Incised Hieroglyphic symbols.

FREDERICK MONDERSON

Deir el Bahari 3b and c. An old photograph shows early efforts of clearing the temple dating to late 19th Century (left); and, from the southwest showing entrance to Mentuhotep's temple (left) and early stages of clearance of Hatshepsut's in the distance.

Deir el Bahari 3d and e. Close-up photograph showing much of the Upper Terrace and Upper Court cleared (left); and, close-up of clearance of the Second Ramp, Upper Terrace and Upper Court.

Deir el Bahari 4. View from the mountain. Hathor Shrine (right), Colonnade of the Upper Court, Second Ramp and Northern Colonnade.

Majestic and alternating eleven columns and pillars in each arrangement are symbolic of Hathor, Goddess of the West. While

HATSHEPSUT'S TEMPLE AT DEIR EL BAHARI

the North Colonnade speaks of things Mythological, the South portrays the inspiration and acquisition of Obelisks at Aswan, set up for the Supreme Majesty of the Land, Lord of Adoration, Amon of Karnak. The Lord of Life is fearful, terrible, great of will and mighty in appearance. He abounds in victuals, creates substance and abides in all things for he is unique in his nature, this godly Bull of the Nine Gods.

The second ascent of the Central Ramp splits your Second Court in rise to the Third Terrace. Abutting this Ramp is the Middle Colonnade.

The Pillared "Birth" and "Coronation" Colonnades to the North and Punt Colonnade to the south of this Middle Colonnade reminds of the august deeds in Hatshepsut's reign. Against the north cliffs, the true Northern Colonnade with 15 columns fronts 4 chapels of worship or accoutrements of the ritual. Subjects of the Birth and Coronation depiction bespeak immortal remembrance and adversaries' enmity for ruler and architect, some say lovers, whose innovation, is a wonderful and splendid architectural and artistic creative work. Senmut praised his majesty Hatshepsut and glorified her master, Amon-Ra, who created the gods and raised up the sky. He is the Lord of Rays who created light.

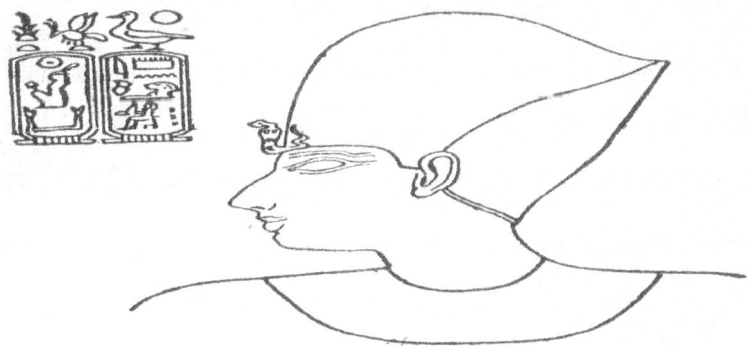

Illustration 4. Profile portrait and Royal Ovals of Queen Hatshepsut wearing Blue or War Crown.

FREDERICK MONDERSON

The Second Ramp's ascent to the Upper Terrace reveal 22 Osiride Figures before pillars fronting columns in similar arrangement where the Third or Upper Open Court and oblong Upper Terrace are surrounded by an enormous colonnade arrangement of 80 columns, all before the Sanctuary. That is before the Portico was erected. North and south Chapels to Hatshepsut and Amon provide meaning to the structure. Northeast and southwest of the Second Court, Chapels to Anubis and Hathor respectively employ twelve and thirty columns with four pillars and each with outer and inner Sanctuary.

In your blessed abode, the Lord of the Ninth Day of the Month Festival in whose honor men keep the Sixth and Seventh Day, the Sole One who made all that is, the One and Only who made all that exists, is perpetually worshiped.

Though his name is hidden from his children, his beauty captivates the heart and love of him makes languid the arms. Love of him makes feeble the arms and his adherents' hearts forget when they look upon him.

Deir el Bahari 5. View of the Amphitheater from the mountain. First and Second Ramp, Second Court, Middle and Upper Colonnade or Terrace, and Upper Court with the Colonnade surrounding the Sanctuary against the mountain face. The Ramp and ruins of Mentuhotep's Temple is in the rear. Clearly, the Queen built a larger Temple than her ancestor and this may have contributed to some of her proscriptions.

August abode, Senmut fashioned your portals to praise his beautiful Queen Hatshepsut. Her father Amon is God extraordinary. His beneficence creates the light, his eye overthrows the enemy, of a

HATSHEPSUT'S TEMPLE AT DEIR EL BAHARI

kind heart Amon, hears the praise of the prisoner. He rescues the fearful from the oppressor and judges between the miserable and strong. These things and more your precinct represents as it withstood the ravages of time. Yet, still, Deir el Bahari retains the power, aura, awe and majesty of its ancient mystique.

Moderns revealed 40 royal mummies in the Deir el-Bahari "cache" and another 153 mummies, in this northern Coptic Convent or Sanatorium of healing. Senmut secreted his tomb and deposited figures of him-self throughout. He decorated, covered, and painted your walls; to foil his adversaries' anticipated destructive acts. Later, when the upper stucco gave way they revealed his artistry, a labor of love.

This and so much more your wonderful majestic structure has represented for Millennia, attesting to the divine inspiration that planned, guided and executed your building in praise of Amon by your mistress and her architect, Senmut.

Deir el Bahari 5a. Erik Monderson and friends on the Upper Terrace before surviving statues of Hatshepsut.

FREDERICK MONDERSON

Deir el Bahari 5b. Another view of Mentuhotep's temple that influenced Senmut's choice and pattern for his Queen's temple with the Chapel of Hathor at the lower center and southern tip of the Upper Court below and the mountain wall right.

3. THE TEMPLE OF DEIR EL BAHARI: An Overview
By
Frederick Monderson

The amphitheater of Deir el-Bahari is overflowing with history, culture, religion, art, architecture, and power, whether spiritual, cosmological, psychological, therapeutic, political and even symbolic. For two thousand years Before the Common Era, this site radiated the intellectual and philosophical dynamism that characterized ancient African thought, practice and artistic expression, in man's early and first conscious awakening. For the two thousand years of the current era, the temple has retained the majesty of that mystique in an art form, whether natural or man-made, and to this day, it continues to mesmerize visitors who are impressed by the scenery and the architectural creations that grace and characterize this holy spot. Thus, Deir el Bahari is one of those sites in the land of ancient Kemet that continues to beckon modern travelers. They continue to be attracted and amazed by the daring and creative genius of ancient Africans who drew back the veil of the mist of antiquity and upon nature's wonderful landscape created

HATSHEPSUT'S TEMPLE AT DEIR EL BAHARI

conventions in art, religion, astronomy, science, building and sincere equality in divine and human relations.

All this rested on the premise of a philosophic axiom of *Ma'at*, the notion of justice, fairness, order, balance, etc. These ideas came to characterize the African personality in an ancient world with civilization just coming into vogue. Herein lies the legacy and heritage of people of African descent who gave so much to the world that the continent came to shape. Yet, thousands of years later, the sons and daughters of these early Africans are victimized in a world that has become too mechanical and materialistic. Perhaps this heritage provided too much fuel for greed, avarice, injustice, disrespect and disunity now plaguing human relations. Nevertheless, to recall, it was Caseley Hayford of Ghana, West Africa, who in 1922, characterized a world gone insane and had become infected with this technological malaise seriously in need of the humanity and forgiving nature of the African personality, possible the only hope to save mankind. That reality has not changed, nearly a century later. Therefore, in this need, the august and powerful cultural and humanistic beginnings inaugurated by Africans along the Nile River, seem the only solution available. That is why so much emphasis need be put on ancient Africa's gifts that manifested first in Ethiopia and then Kemet/Egypt, mother Africa's oldest daughters. We need tell the youngsters, as Afrocentrists would argue the foundation of African historiographic reconstruction rests in knowledge of this powerful legacy.

Illustration 5. First ship of outgoing squadron bound for Punt. (From Mariette's *Deir el Bahari*, plate 12.)

FREDERICK MONDERSON

In this unfolding, both African men and women have played meaningful roles and in the assignment of reclaiming the ancient heritage it will take all of us for our people to be able to overcome and progress. So, we must study Egypt, teach grandparents, parents, aunts and uncles, neighbors and all who will listen and seek knowledge. Egypt is the Key! This is indeed a powerful task! A trip to the land of ancient Kemet, modern Egypt and exposure to the monuments, go a long way of creating visual images challenging the cognitive faculties to imbibe in a wonderful intellectual adventure. Such is guaranteed to change personal views of themselves, their ancestors and in process strengthen their resolve for the challenges that lie ahead.

Deir el Bahari 5c– The God and the King, Queen Hatshepsut on the same level. They both have "tails."

Deir el Bahari – Under architrave decoration.

HATSHEPSUT'S TEMPLE AT DEIR EL BAHARI

Deir el Bahari 6. View from the Mountain. Broken columns of the Colonnade of the Upper Court, Second Ramp and ruins of Mentuhotep's Temple to the right.

As I penned this correspondence, I was also thinking about my grandson Men-Kheper-ra who was christened on a Sunday in October in 1999. We held a reception at our home after the service in church. Like most parents with some sense of a vision of the future, I wondered what would happen to him and his generation. I was therefore convinced that writings of this nature would help to strengthen him as he, too, learns about the role of the ancestors of ancient Kemet/Egypt. Believe me, that is exactly why I asked his parents to name him after the great 18th Dynasty Pharaoh Thutmose III, *Men-Kheper-Ra* who was not simply a king, but also a mighty warrior, builder, administrator and equally devoutly religious. Yet, in all of this the great king had a feud with, some scholars say, his half-sister, wife, aunt, Queen Hatshepsut. Even families have their differences. This is what Breasted called "The Feud of the Tuthmosids!" History can teach us so much, nevertheless!

FREDERICK MONDERSON

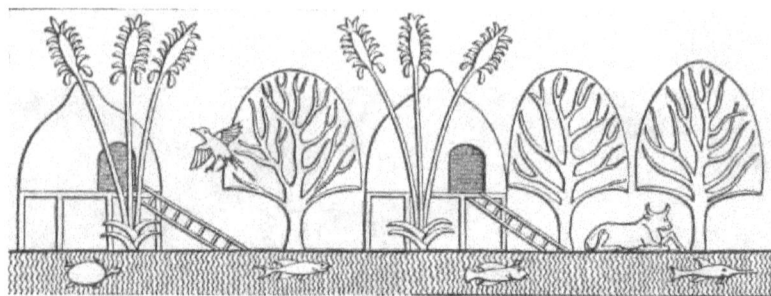

Illustration 6. View of a Village in Punt. (From Mariette's *Deir-El-Bahari*, Plate 5.) The huts of the natives are built on piles and approached by ladders, and, according to Dumichen, closely resemble the Toguls of the modern Soudanese. The trees are two Date palms in fruit, and three myrrh-trees (odiferous sycamore), the foliage of the latter being indicated by a line bounding the tops of the branches. The bird flying to left is identified with the *Cinnyris Metallica*, a native of the Somali country, having two long tail-feathers of which only one has been given by the ancient Egyptian artist.

Deir el Bahari 6a. Looking beyond the mountain to the flat-land with the Ramesseum in the center and riverain greenery in rear.

HATSHEPSUT'S TEMPLE AT DEIR EL BAHARI

4. "AN IMPORTANT ARCHAEOLOGICAL DISCOVERY IN EGYPT" was reported in *Nature* (June 16, 1904: 55-57).

"The most important archaeological event reported from Egypt during the last excavation season (1903-4) is the discovery by Prof. Naville, of the University of Geneva, and Mr. H.R. Hall, of the British Museum, of the most ancient temple at Thebes. Messrs. Naville and Hall on behalf of the Egypt Exploration Fund carried on the excavations, which is to be congratulated on having made this important discovery. The services, which have been rendered by the Egypt Exploration Fund to Egyptological science since its foundation, some twenty years ago, have indeed been innumerable.

Deir el Bahari 7. View from the mountain. Most buses terminate further east at that rest house. The gases from motorized vehicles have been damaging the monuments.

"One of the most important works carried out by the fund was Prof. Naville's complete excavation of the great temple of Deir el-Bahari, in the western hills of Thebes. The excavation came to an end in 1899, after the main temple had been entirely cleared and the necessary works of conservation and restoration had been carried out, but before the environs of the temple had been completely explored. To the south of the temple lay a wilderness of rubbish heaps, which might conceal a necropolis or even another temple, placed between the great shrine built by Queen Hatshepsut and the southern horn of the *cirque* of cliffs which rise behind and around Deir el-Bahari. Means for further excavation failed, however, and the exploration of the un-excavated tract to the south of the temple was postponed until the present season, when Prof. Naville again took up the spade and very soon discovered that underneath the heaps of rubbish lay the not inconsiderable remains of a smaller temple, of high archaeological importance on account of its age. It is the funerary temple or mortuary chapel of the most distinguished monarch of the eleventh dynasty, Nebkherura Mentuhetep, who reigned about 2500 B.C., according to the best authorities. A temple of this date is a great rarity in Egypt. The new temple, however, comes *next* to them in age, and if they surpass it in peculiarities of architecture, it appears to fully equal them in general architectural interest and to surpass them in the point of artistic interest and importance, since it has added considerably to our knowledge of the history of Egyptian art.

Deir el Bahari 7a. Neter, Scepter, Hare and Christian Cross symbolism.

HATSHEPSUT'S TEMPLE AT DEIR EL BAHARI

Deir el Bahari 7b. Erik Monderson stands in the Court beside the *in situ* altar of Ra-Horakhti's Chapel comprised of 10 steps.

Illustration 7. The Royal Envoy, attended by his bodyguard, display the gifts sent by Hatasu to the Prince of Punt. (From Mariette's *Deir el Bahari*, plate 5.)

FREDERICK MONDERSON

The artistic triumphs of the Old Empire are well-known. But our knowledge of the condition of art at the beginning of the Middle Empire under the eleventh dynasty was, until the present discovery, scanty. The general impression has been that the work of the eleventh dynasty was rough and crude in style. The discovery in the new temple at Deir el-Bahari of hundreds of fragments of colored relief sculptures of the eleventh dynasty compels us to modify this impression, and we see from them that, side by side with the somewhat crude and awkward productions hitherto considered characteristic of this dynasty, work of the highest excellence was also turned out.

This is an important result, and it is by no means improbable that this improved artistic style is the work of a sculptor who, we know, lived in the reign of Nebkherura, Mertisen by name, and his school.

Deir el Bahari 7c. Another mountain view of the old staging area for buses before the First Pylon entrance to the Temple.

HATSHEPSUT'S TEMPLE AT DEIR EL BAHARI

Deir el Bahari 7d. Close up view of the Second Ramp, Upper Terrace and upper Court of the Temple against the mountain with ruins of Mentuhotep's Middle Kingdom Temple further on.

Deir el Bahari 7e. Another close up of the Upper Terrace and Upper Court showing the Sanctuary's entrance overhead escarpment indicative of being tunneled into the surrounding7 mountain that serves as a backdrop.

FREDERICK MONDERSON

Deir el Bahari 8. Mountain view of the two Ramps and Lower, Middle and Upper Colonnade against the mountain back-drop.

Deir el Bahari 8a. Coming down the mountain the two ramps, Lower, Middle and Upper Colonnades become clearer.

These reliefs originally formed part of the decoration of the walls of the main pillared hall of Nebkherura's temple. This hall, only a part of which has as yet been uncovered, stands upon an artificially squared platform of rock, immediately to the south of the Hathor Shrine of the great temple of Deir el-Bahari, and separated from it by a small open court about sixty feet across. The platform is about fifteen feet high.

HATSHEPSUT'S TEMPLE AT DEIR EL BAHARI

Its sides were masked by a magnificent wall of finely squared and fitted limestone blocks, built in bonded courses of broad and narrow blocks alternately, one above the other, as may be seen from the photograph. In the extreme South West corner of the court this wall is perfect. It is without doubt one of the finest specimens of Egyptian masonry yet brought to light. Entrance to the main hall on the platform was gained, as in the great temple, by means of an inclined ramp, which led up to an entrance gate, no doubt, like that of the main temple, a trilithon of red granite; the threshold of finely-polished red granite still remains *in situ*. The socket in which the door turned (in the usual ancient manner before the invention of...) is clearly seen, and also small side run, or channel, by which the door could be bodily removed from the socket and replaced when necessary. To the north of the ramp a colonnade of small, square sandstone pillars has been discovered, placed on a stone pavement immediately before and below the platform. It can hardly be doubted that a second similar colonnade originally existed south of the ramp. Thus, we have the main portion consisting of a pillared, or "hypostyle," hall of octagonal pillars placed on a platform of rock, approached by an inclined ramp, flanked by colonnades on the lowly ground level. It will be noticed by all who have visited Deir el-Bahari that, so far as platform, ramp, and colonnades are concerned, this is precisely the arrangement of the great temple of Queen Hatshepsut, or Hatasu, to the north [as] it opens up a new field of possibilities. The curious plan of the great temple has puzzled archaeologists and architects from Wilkinson's time to the present day. Whence this curious arrangement of platforms, inclined planes, and colonnades, is totally unlike anything else in Egypt? Various theories have been propounded, but it is only now that the solution has been found, owing to the discovery of the temple Nebkherura.

Colonnades, platforms, and ramps are then a feature of the older temple-architecture of Egypt; they were, at the time of the eighteenth dynasty, when the great temple of Hatshepsut was built, old-fashioned, archaic, but it is evident that the great temple, is as far as its main arrangements are concerned, a mere enlarged copy of the thousand-year older temple at its side; it is simply a "magnificent archaism."

When it was built the older and smaller temple was still used as a temple, apparently, and both existed side by side for some time; this is shown by the fact that the later temple is not placed in the center of the cirque but is crammed against the northern cliff-face, it could not be placed in the center because the southern portion of the space at Deir el-Bahari was already occupied by the older temple. It was built roughly parallel to the older temple; it is oriented 24 degrees S of E (Lockyer, *Dawn of Astronomy*, p. 212), and this must be more or less the orientation of Nebkherura's temple also. This fact is of interest, as the question might be mooted whether the orientation of the main temple is also an archaism imitated from the Nebkherura's temple (B.C. 2500), or not. Sir Norman Lockyer has postulated (*Dawn of Astronomy*, p. 218) the existence in the western hills at Thebes of a temple of Hathor older than the shrine of the goddess at Deir el-Bahari: "built to observe the rising of the star [Hathor-Sothis, i.e., Sirius] at a time, perhaps somewhat later than that given by Biot (3200 B.C.)." Nebkherura's date is about 2500 B.C., but we have as yet no proof that in his funerary temple the reverence paid to his spirit was conjoined with a worship of Hathor. We may find this proof in the course of the further excavations or of the older temple of Hathor may have existed further to the southward, perhaps on the site of the present little temple dedicated to Hathor or the Waste at Deir el-Medina, which was originally founded in the reign of Amenhetep III, B.C. 1450. Certain it is that the worship of Hathor in the western hills is far older than the time of Amenhetep III and Hatshepsut, and the foundation of the oldest temple built in her honor at Deir el-Bahari or Deir el-Medina may well go back to very near the date propounded by Biot for the systematic observation of the helical rising of Sothis-Hathor (Sirius).

HATSHEPSUT'S TEMPLE AT DEIR EL BAHARI

Deir el Bahari 10. Newly opened entrance to the Sanctuary.
It is to this very period-between 3285 B.C. and 2400 B.C. that the beginnings of the Theban Empire and of the Theban temples must be placed. To the student of the astronomical orientation of Egyptian temples the new discovery will, therefore, be of the highest interest.

Among the large number of smaller objects discovered in the course of the excavations, the most interesting will probably prove to be the series of small ex-votos of devotees of Hathor, found in the court between the two temples. These consist of small cows (the sacred animal of the goddess), and female figures in earthenware and blue faience, votive eyes and ears in bronze and faience, broken blue vases with representations of the holy cow emblazoned with stars, &c.

These votive offerings, which nearly date to the eighteenth dynasty, were undoubtedly originally devoted in the Hathor shrine of the great temple, and when the shrine became too full was thrown down by the sacristans into the space between the two temples, which thus became a dust-heap. And from this dust-heap many interesting objects have been recovered, including a copper chisel with hardened edge, which should be of special interest to metallurgists, and specimens of palm-fruit, nuts, reeds, and shells, dating to about 1500 B.C. One of the most remarkable objects found is a perfect three-cornered loaf of unleavened bread, of the same date. All these smaller objects, together with a number of specimens of the eleventh dynasty reliefs already described, will, we understand, be exhibited at the annual exhibition of the Egypt Exploration Fund at University College, Gower Street, in July next.

Subscriptions for the work of the Egypt Exploration Fund are much needed, and should be sent to the Secretary, 37 Great Russell Street, W.C. We are indebted to Mr. Hall for the photographs here published."

Illustration 8. Procession of the Prince of Punt, accompanied by his wife, family and followers. (From Mariette's *Deir el-Bahari*, plate 5.)

Illustration 9. Men carrying saplings of the "Ana-sycamore" in baskets, from the shore to the ships. (From Mariette's *Deir el-Bahari*, plate 5.)

HATSHEPSUT'S TEMPLE AT DEIR EL BAHARI

5. THE TEMPLE OF DEIR EL BAHARI: An Introduction
By
Frederick Monderson

The temple of Deir el-Bahari, *Djeser Djeseru* (*Sacred of Sacreds*) is a magnificent specimen of ancient Egyptian architecture of the 18th Dynasty, New Kingdom. It is constructed of white limestone that looks like white marble and, according to Breasted it's been called "most splendid" and "The temple of myriad of years; its great doors fashioned of black copper, the inlaid figures of electrum." Further it's been called *khikhet*, "the great seat of Amon, his horizon in the west, all its doors of real cedar wrought with bronze." Equally, it's a "Horizon of the God Amun." An inscription states it was built by the "Good God Ramaka, beloved of Amun in Servi" and of the "house of Amon, his enduring 0horizon of eternity; its floors wrought with gold and silver, its beauty was like the horizon of heaven." Today it is a featured tourist attraction in the land of ancient monuments that so fascinates the modern mindset. However, Deir el-Bahari, the modern name, also "the northern convent" is different than most other temples of this culture. Beyond being an architectural masterpiece, it is about a famous queen, her very astute architect, both victimized because of a family feud. It has important historical references to the queen's virgin birth, her expedition to the Land of Punt (on the east African coast near Somali and Ethiopia), and a record of her two obelisks given to the God Amon that were quarried from Aswan stone. It also has frescoes depicting birds in nets and men fishing. It tells the story of the Queen's "virgin birth." It is associated with her father Thutmose I, Amon, Ra-Horakhty, Hathor and Anubis.

Many other gods are represented in this temple. A great replica of an even more ancient temple, it is built in a unique location. It was one of the earliest "3-story buildings" in history and in later times it was a sanatorium. It was occupied by Coptic monks and so became "the convent of the north." The goddess Hathor, whose shrine is located to the south of the main buildings, is often depicted in the illustrations as "coming out of the mountains of Deir el Bahari." Anubis, the god of the dead, has a shrine to the north of the main buildings in the Second Court. The god of the dead and his shrine in this location may be connected to the fact; the belief system holds, when the deceased begins the journey into the afterlife, he enters through a cavern in the Deir el-Bahari vicinity. Interestingly, Thutmose III is shown in an illustration presenting to Sokar, a god of the dead (who looks like Ra-Horakhty and Horus) but he does not have a shrine here. Between the older Mentuhotep temple and that of Hatshepsut, Thutmose III erected his smaller temple. However, being a mortuary temple, having a shrine to the god of the dead, Anubis, in the vicinity of the cavern that entrances the other world may have had some considerations when the priests of the XXIInd Dynasty hid the mummies of the New Kingdom monarchs, discovered there in 1881.

Illustration 10. Gifts presented to the royal envoy by the Prince of Punt. (From Mariette's *Deir el Bahari*, plate 5.)

Invoking cosmological connotations, John Anthony West in *The Traveler's Key to Ancient Egypt* (1995: 350) says: "Suzanne Ratie sees the temple as an expression of the Primordial Hill, its levels corresponding to degrees of spiritualization. It is interesting, if this observation is true, to know that the upper or most spiritualized level was used as a Christian monastery – some say convent." Nevertheless, from the time travelers began to trek up the Nile River, many explorers visited Deir el-Bahari from as early as its discovery in 1743, and several archaeologists and Egyptologists worked this site. The Egypt Exploration Fund began excavation of

HATSHEPSUT'S TEMPLE AT DEIR EL BAHARI

the temple, *Amon in Teren*, oriented on a southeast and northwest axis, under Edouard Naville in 1893 and then Americans began restoration in 1911. From 1961 a Polish team began restoration of the Upper Platform that was only finished a few years ago. Important, however, is the use and arrangement of columns and pillars in this wonderful structure.

Deir el Bahari 10a. Another of those images of the Queen, this time wearing the Red Crown, that have escaped the wrath of her adversaries. Her Ka accompanies the Queen.

The approach to the temple is from a Valley Temple at the river's edge that is now destroyed. Here they found foundation deposits, alabaster jars and model adzes. Blocks from walls found here named Puyemre as architect. Bricks with names of Hatshepsut and Thutmose I and also of Hatshepsut and Princess Neferure have been found as well as an alabaster dish with inscriptions regarding the Great Temple. Blocks of the Queen being crowned and sandstone name-stones of her also were found in vicinity of the Valley Temple.

Deir el Bahari 11. Thutmose III, Men-Khepper-Ra (Cartouche, Shennu) and a female, presumably the Queen or Hathor. Both faces are defaced.

The temple's approach led along a Sphinx-lined Causeway leading to the Bark-station for the God Amon before the Entrance Pylon. Before this pylon were planted two Persea incense trees (*Mimusops Schimperi*), brought from Punt to which the Queen sent Nehsi, Senmut and another of her loyal subjects on an historic expedition. Flanking the Causeway and in the First Court were beds of flowers,

HATSHEPSUT'S TEMPLE AT DEIR EL BAHARI

palm and papyrus reeds, pools and statues. Evidence shows there were 4 ponds of water in the neighborhood called "the ponds of milk" for the God Amun to cool off in as he walked around his garden. After all, Deir el Bahari was to be a paradise for Amun even though there were a multitude of other gods who shared this beautiful holy place. Off to the right, from the western end of the Court, the Northern Colonnade formed part of the retaining wall.

Deir el Bahari 11a. The "Prince of the City" according to Ludwig Burchardt.

The Lower Colonnade in the First Court is divided by the First Ramp. To the south is the Obelisk Colonnade showing, according to Porter and Moss (1972: 342) two: "Ships bringing obelisks, including bull, sphinx and lion, in cages; processions of soldiers, including archers, standard-bearers, trumpeter, drummer and ritual-scene with priests and butchers." The left ship has the obelisks and the right ship shows rowers. There is also a caged lion, and a group of soldiers on the prow of the right ship. An ox is sacrificed and "Tables of Offerings" to the Theban deities are laid out before the troops. There are four scenes showing Hatshepsut offering the obelisks to Amon, she running with a vase to Amon, the Goddess Sheshat and the Queen offering the temple to Amon. To the north of this Lower Colonnade scenes of fowling and fishing, with the Queen in a canoe and birds and waterfowls drawn by two gods.

FREDERICK MONDERSON

There are also scenes of waterfowls in nets, the queen offering five royal statues to Amon and driving four calves to Amon. She is also shown as a sphinx trampling upon her foes. The pillars contain fragments with hawk and royal titles. There is a royal statue in a boat as well as a fragment of a text of Hatshepsut's Syrian campaign that also mentions Thutmose I. A lion is shown at the base of the First Ramp leading to the Second Court. The Lower Colonnade has 1 row of 11 pillars in front and 1 row of 11 sixteen-sided columns behind each on both the north and south divided by the First Ramp. The number 11 is special to the Goddess Hathor and so too is the number 7.

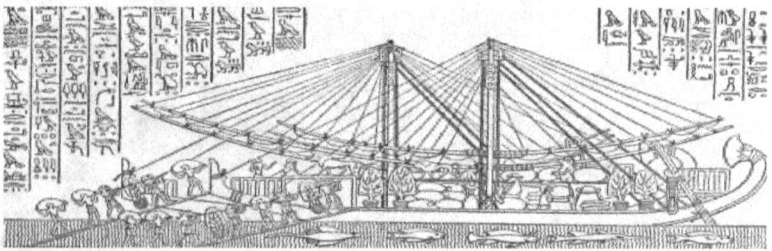

Illustration 11. A Ship of the Egyptian squadron being laden with products from Punt. (From Mariette's *Deir el-Bahari*, Plate 5.)

The Second Court houses the Middle Colonnade that has 2 rows of 11 pillars inside and outside, again split by the Second Ramp (for 44) along whose balustrade is a coiled serpent with a protective hawk. In this Second Court was found a temple to Amenhotep I and his mother Queen Aahmes-Nefertari, Hatshepsut's grandfather and great-grandmother. Senmut destroyed this temple in building his own. To the right of this Second Court, Senmut's tomb was discovered. Bricks with the names of Queen Aahmes Nefertari and her son were found and some re-used while others were dispersed to museums. Porter and Moss mention a Brick Shrine to Aesculapius (Imhotep) that was destroyed.

HATSHEPSUT'S TEMPLE AT DEIR EL BAHARI

Deir el Bahari 12. Another close-up of Nubians in the temple.

On the south is the Punt Colonnade, depicting the 5 ships in the trading expedition to the land of Punt in Central East Africa. Baikie (1932: 420) quotes Breasted stating the Queen explained: "'A command was heard from the great throne, an oracle of the god himself that the ways to Punt should be searched out, that the highways to the Myrrh-trees should be penetrated.' There had, of course, been several previous expeditions to Punt; one sent by Sahure in the Vth Dynasty, and another by Isesi of the same dynasty, which brought back a pygmy dancer. In the VIth Dynasty one of the officials of Pepi II was killed by Arabs while superintending the building of a ship for the voyage, and a second expedition was made in the same reign; in the Middle Kingdom Henu conducted an expedition for Mentuhotpe III, and other voyages were made under Amenemhet II and Senusret II of the XIIth Dynasty." However, none of these expeditions were as graphic as Hatshepsut's and this is why her work affixed to the temple makes it even more interesting.

The walls of this Punt Colonnade has six registers that depict, Porter and Moss (1994: 344) note: "Cattle, rhinoceros facing baboon with its young, and men carrying incense-trees; Giraffe, trees felled and men with ebony logs; men with incense-trees; Village of Punt with huts and ladders, cattle, two men with asses, two men with tribute, Parahu, Chief of Punt with wife Ity 'Queen of Punt,' and man with tribute, heap of treasure, received by Egyptian officer, and text; village with huts and ladders, incense-trees, three men, Queen riding ass, Chief of Punt, 'Queen,' and attendants, with text and treasure received by Egyptian officer and nine soldiers." In addition, the Queen is shown "consecrating two registers of products of Punt. Giraffe, panther, leopard, skins, and weighing-scene of Dedwen, Horus and [Seshat] writing on palette; incense-trees, cattle grazing, and treasure, incense-trees in pots, men measuring heaps of incense, and [Thoth] writing on palette." Elsewhere, giraffe and leopards, panther and leopards, scales and gold-rings; Queen with staff and Punt Expedition text before Amon. South of the Punt Colonnade, the Hathor Shrine or southern speos, has 1 row of 4 pillars with Hathor Head capitals up front and another row of 4 that splits 4 more rows of 6 similarly disposed sixteen-sided columns of "Proto-Doric" type in a greater collection. There are 2 more round columns near the Sanctuary. Thus, in this Hathor Shrine there are pillars and round columns with Hathor Head Capitals that have a female face or head with cow's ears and sistrums or rattles, the goddess' symbols. There is also a second type of column, sixteen-sided. This arrangement blends three types of column and pillar helps to convey the notion of genius at work.

Illustration 12. Tributaries of Punt walking in the Procession to the Temple of Amen. (From Mariette's *Deir el Bahari*.)

On the north is the Birth Colonnade and further right of this is the Anubis Shrine with 3 rows of 4 each sixteen-sided 'Proto-Doric' columns. The Anubis shrine or northern speos with a Hypostyle Hall

HATSHEPSUT'S TEMPLE AT DEIR EL BAHARI

has much color in wonderfully preserved reliefs depicting the importance of this God of the Dead. Much of the Birth Colonnade has been destroyed through erasure, though the coronation of the queen is very apparent. Porter and Moss (1972: 347) mention a number of scenes including Hatshepsut being "purified by Ra-Horakhty and Amon and Amon presenting Queen as child to gods of the south and north." There is a "Long text of Queen's journey with Tuthmose I, and two scenes, [Queen] led by [goddess] and Hathor, followed by [Khnum and divinities], to Atum, [presentation of crowns to Queen] with Seshet and [Thoth] writing Queen's name on palettes, both seated; Queen [as king] greeted by Inmutf before Amon, and behind her three rows of gods of the southern chapel and gods of the southern and northern shrines, with Seshet and Thoth, both seated, writing on palettes …. Queen crowned by Thutmose I in the presence of nine officials, with long speeches of the King and Queen." Three more scenes show the Queen led by Inmutf, purified by Ha of Sheta and led by Horus. Two scenes show "Horus and Seth crowning the Queen with white and red crown, and Queen preceded by standards of Thoth, Horus, Khons and Anubis."

Deir el Bahari 12a. Erik Monderson stands to the left of the Portico entrance to the Sanctuary in the Upper Court. The openings are for Niches of the Queen, since lost.

FREDERICK MONDERSON

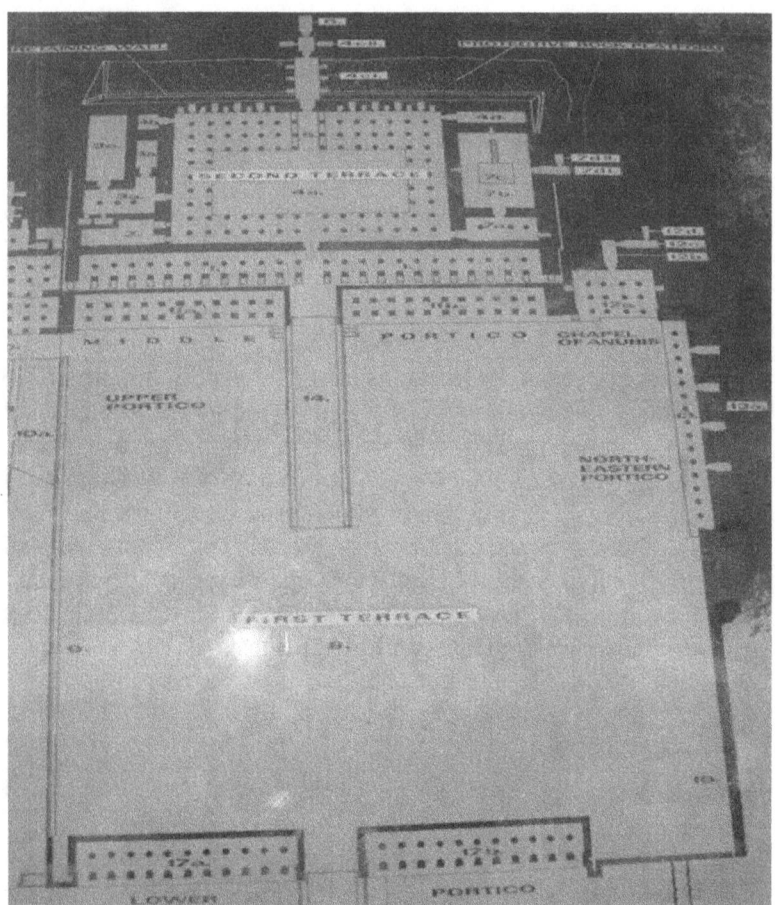

Deir el Bahari 12b. Plan of the temple from the Lower to the Upper Colonnade.

In the lower register there are birth-scenes with Hatshepsut's mother Queen Ahmosi and children, the Ennead before Amon, and names of various gods. Then there are seven scenes that Porter and Moss (1972: 348) mention as: "Amon and Thoth facing each other; Thoth led by Amon; Queen Ahmosi receiving life from Amon, both seated, upheld by two goddesses seated on lion-couch; Amon and Khnum facing each other; Heket kneeling, offering life to children

HATSHEPSUT'S TEMPLE AT DEIR EL BAHARI

modeled by Khnum; Thoth with Queen Ahmosi; Queen Ahmosi led to Birth-room by Heket and Khnum."

Illustration 13. Procession of the Queen. Her Majesty's fan-bearers, quiver-bearer, sandal-bearer, and grooms with hunting leopards. (From Mariette's *Deir el Bahari*.)

Deir el Bahari 12c. Hatshepsut kneels to present two oil vases to Amon Ra in the temple's Sanctuary.

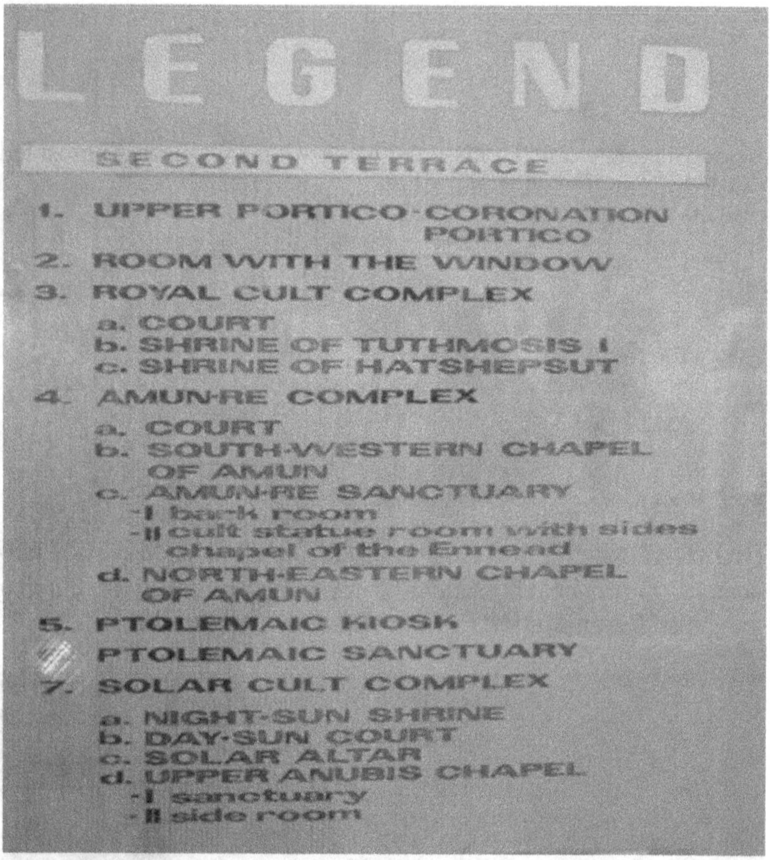

FREDERICK MONDERSON

LEGEND

SECOND TERRACE

1. UPPER PORTICO-CORONATION PORTICO
2. ROOM WITH THE WINDOW
3. ROYAL CULT COMPLEX
   a. COURT
   b. SHRINE OF TUTHMOSIS I
   c. SHRINE OF HATSHEPSUT
4. AMUN-RE COMPLEX
   a. COURT
   b. SOUTH-WESTERN CHAPEL OF AMUN
   c. AMUN-RE SANCTUARY
      - I back room
      - II cult statue room with sides chapel of the Ennead
   d. NORTH-EASTERN CHAPEL OF AMUN
5. PTOLEMAIC KIOSK
6. PTOLEMAIC SANCTUARY
7. SOLAR CULT COMPLEX
   a. NIGHT-SUN SHRINE
   b. DAY-SUN COURT
   c. SOLAR ALTAR
   d. UPPER ANUBIS CHAPEL
      - I sanctuary
      - II side room

Deir el Bahari 12d. Legend illustrating the upper regions of the temple outward.

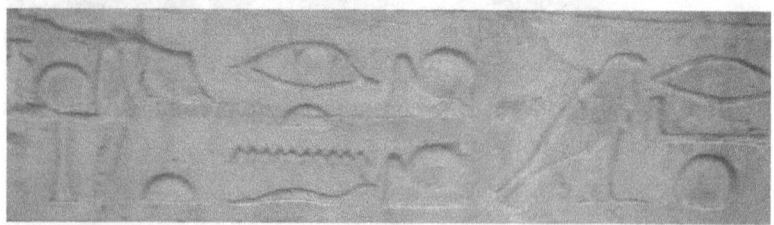

Deir el Bahari 12e– More under architrave decoration.

HATSHEPSUT'S TEMPLE AT DEIR EL BAHARI

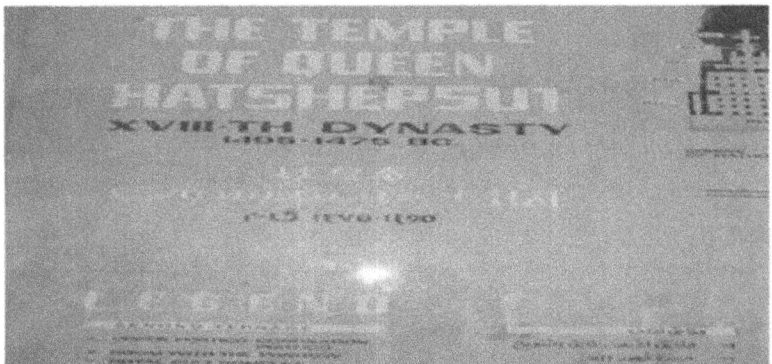

Deir el Bahari 12f. Graphic showing the temple's name and period of its owner's reign.

Even further, Porter and Moss (1972: 348) say another register tells of the: "Birth-scene in the presence of three rows of divinities (two rows on lion couches), including three kneeling figures of Heket, Souls of Pe and Nekhen, two figures of Heh supporting zed-pillar, Bes and Tueris, with Amon, followed by divinities on left and Meskhenet on right." In addition, Porter and Moss (1972: 349) continued: "Three scenes show Amon before Hathor seated holding child; facing Hathor seated, with [goddess] and Selkis beyond; Queen Ahmosi suckling child, with attendant and two cow-headed goddesses suckling children [Hatshepsut and her ka], all on lion-couch with cows below, and nine divinities nursing children beyond."

Much further, the illustrations indicate two scenes show: "The children presented by Hapi and the milk god Iat (neither named) to three seated Osiride gods, [children] presented by Thoth to Amon. Khnum and Anubis with disk on left, Seshet writing and Hapi on right, establish the child's length of reign, and two rows in center, each with two kneeling goddesses and the children, with a kneeling god (in upper row), and a kneeling woman (in lower row, holding inkpot for Seshet)."

FREDERICK MONDERSON

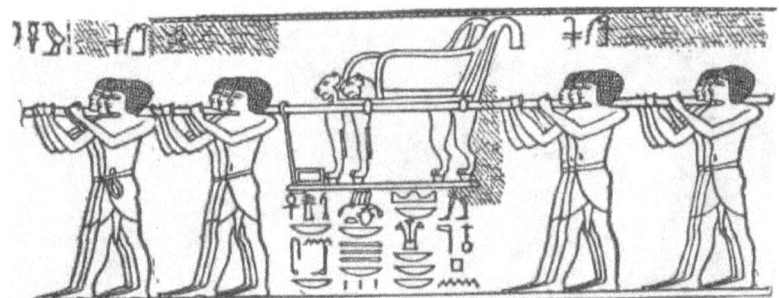

Illustration 14. Her Majesty's throne-chair carried by twelve bearers. (From Mariette's *Deir el-Bahari*.)

Just east of the Anubis Shrine, the Northern Colonnade has 15 remaining columns, seeming to indicate this part of the temple was unfinished.

Illustration 15. Ceremony supposed to take place in the temple of Amen at Karnak. (From Mariette's *Deir el-Bahari*.)

The Upper Terrace houses the Upper Colonnade, comprising 11 pillars in front and 11 sixteen-sided columns behind, on both north and south sides split by the granite trilithon doorway or gate that entrances from the Upper Terrace to the Upper Court beyond. In front of the pillars were Osiride Figures or statues of the Queen and this is particularly visible from the Bird's Eye View on the mountain when you look towards this Upper Terrace.

HATSHEPSUT'S TEMPLE AT DEIR EL BAHARI

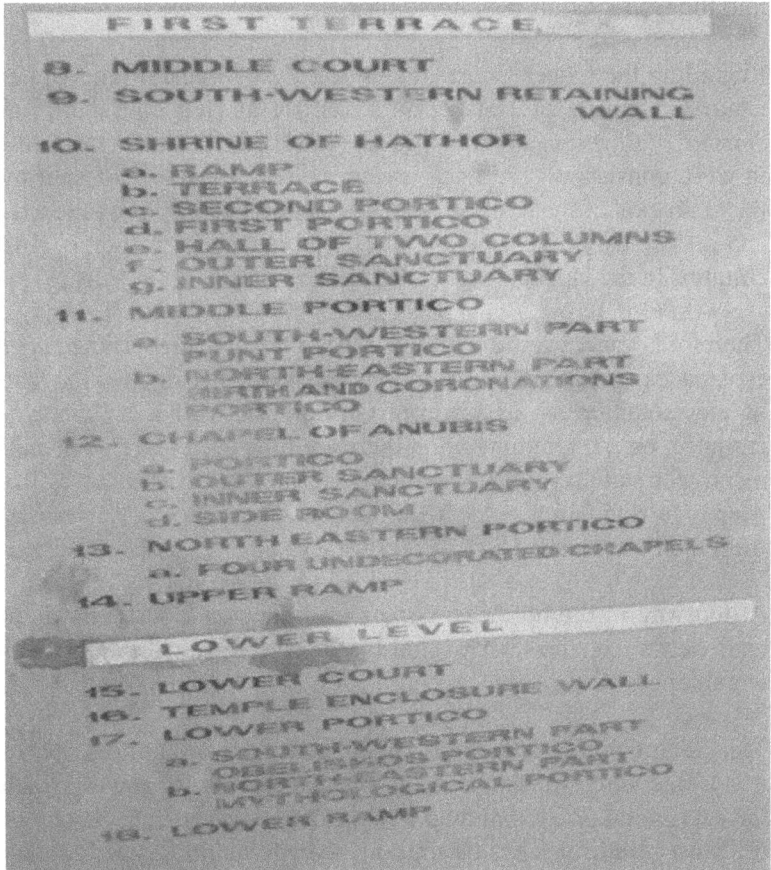

Deir el Bahari 12g. Second part of the Legend showing the outer features of the temple towards the east.

The Upper Court beyond the Upper Terrace where the Sanctuary is located against the face of the mountain has a wonderful arrangement of columns surrounding the Open Court. On the Upper Terrace, Baikie (1932: 424) informs: "A colonnade formerly ran along the face of this court, on the upper level. It consisted of two rows, the front one of twenty-two Osiride statues of Hatshepsut, subsequently converted into square pillars by Tuthmosis III, the

FREDERICK MONDERSON

back row of the same number of sixteen-sided columns." In addition, a pillar and column support the granite gateway entrance into the Upper Court beyond.

Regarding the Upper Court Colonnade, Z. Winsock's "The Upper Court Colonnade of Hatshepsut's Temple at Deir el Bahari," in *Journal of Egyptian Archaeology* 66 (1980: 55) illustrates from east to west, consists of 2 in front and to the rear 4 rows of 14 split by the main axis of the temple; then 3 rows of 8 again split by the axis and all enclosing the Open Court. This makes for a total of 108 columns in the Upper Court Colonnade.

Therefore, on entering the Court, the Colonnade arrangement esplanades and encompasses the Ptolemaic Portico against the face of the mountain as a backdrop. On both sides of the Sanctuary entrance, on the retaining wall, there are nine each large and small niches for statues, many of which were broken by Thutmose III's people in retaliation against the Queen. The Sanctuary is closed from the Portico area.

A doorway in the northeast corner of the Upper Court's northern wall leads to the Solar Courtyard where Ra-Horakhty was worshipped.

This Solar Courtyard, Hall (1910: 465) explained: "In the center of it is a fine white limestone Altar of great size, to the top of which the sacrificing priest mounted a flight of [10] steps. This is one of the most beautiful relics of antiquity ever found in Egypt, and that the Egyptians themselves admired it is shown by the inscription running round it, which states that it was made in honor of the god Ra-Harmachis, 'a great altar of beautiful white stone of Anu.' It was discovered in place by Naville. North of the altar is a mortuary chapel ... cut out of the rock, the paintings on the walls of which are as fresh and brilliant as if they had been executed yesterday. The chapel was dedicated to the memory of Thothmes I and his mother Sen-Seneb. On the right (E) side of this little chapel the obliterations of the queen made by order of Thothmes III are quite different in appearance from those of the god Amen made by order

HATSHEPSUT'S TEMPLE AT DEIR EL BAHARI

of Khu-n-Aten. The former is chiseled out, the latter battered out by a hammer."

Another doorway at the northwest end of this same northern wall leads to the 'North-west Amon Chapel." In the opposite direction at the other end of the court is the "South-west Amon Chapel."

A doorway in the southeast corner of the southern wall leads to the Appearance Chamber and Appearance Lodge. To the right of this another doorway against the southwest of the southern wall leads to a vestibule with 3 columns. To the right of this enclosure is the Thutmose Chapel and to the left the Hatshepsut Chapel. Naturally, the Queen's chapel is larger than Thutmose's.

These areas right and left of the Upper Court are restricted and closed to visitors. To the left or south, Karl Baedeker (1929: 322) describes the H. Room in which: "The ceiling is well preserved. On the right wall appears Amon-re in front of a table of offerings, which replaces the effaced figure of Hatshepsut. Behind the table is the queen's guardian spirit. On the rear wall are Thutmosis III and Thutmosis I (substituted for the queen) making an offering of clothes to Amun. On the left wall Thutmosis II (substituted for the queen), with his guardian spirit, offers sacred oil to the ithyphallic Amun."

On the right of the Upper Court behind the Ra-Horakhty Chapel, again Baedeker (1929: 322) describes the Hall of Amun. "Part of the ceiling, decorated with stars on a blue ground, still remains. On the left side-wall we observe Hatshepsut pacing out of the temple precinct, before Amun, before the ithyphallic Amon-Min, and before the enthroned Amun. On the right wall is Thutmosis III before these same gods. On the rear wall is Thutmosis II (originally Hatshepsut) before Amun. The figures of the gods here were defaced by Amenophis IV, and were not replaced at the restoration under Rameses II."

There are roughly 296 pillars and columns in this temple.

FREDERICK MONDERSON

The Sanctuary rests against the retaining wall, along both sides of which are the niches containing statues of the Queen and even of Senmut, her builder.

Further, in the center, the Greeks built a Portico that entrances the Sanctuary. Baikie (1932: 426) described the Sanctuary that, even though this area of the Upper Court is open to visitors after the Polish Expedition restoration, the Sanctuary itself is closed by a gate and padlock. In 2018 the Sanctuary was opened to visitors. He says: "The entrance to the sanctuary is by a granite doorway in the middle of the west wall. This is approached by a Ptolemaic portico, and is adorned with much defaced reliefs. The sacred shrine has three chambers. On the southern wall of the first, at the foot, is a scene of the temple garden, with birds flying about papyrus thickets, and ducks and fish swimming in a piece of ornamental water. Above, Hatshepsut and her daughter Neferure, making offering to the barque of Amen-Re. On the opposite wall, Hatshepsut, Tuthmosis III and the Princess Neferure offer to the boat, behind which stand defaced figures of Tuthmosis I, Queen Ahmose, and the little princess Bit-Nefru. The second chamber has nothing to note; but the sanctuary, … was taken over by the Ptolemaic artists, who decorated it with two processions of gods – those on the right-hand wall being led by Amenhotep, son of Hapu, the deified factotum of Amenophis III, and those on the left hand by Imhotep, who occupied a similar position in the reign of Zoser (IIIrd Dynasty) and shared the same destiny. The contrast between the delicate and beautiful work of the XVIIIth Dynasty to which we have grown accustomed, and the clumsy and ill-proportioned figures of the Ptolemaic artists, with their bulging muscles and rolls of fat, could not be better exhibited than here, where the Ptolemaic work is seen in close relationship with that of Hatshepsut."

Milne, in "The Sanatorium at Deir el Bahari" (1914: 96) tells: "In Ptolemaic times the upper terrace of the temple of Hatshepsut at Deir el Bahari was given up to the worship of two Egyptian deified heroes – Amenhotep, the son of Hapu, a sage of the New Kingdom, and Imhotep, according to legend a son of Ptah: and under Ptolemy

HATSHEPSUT'S TEMPLE AT DEIR EL BAHARI

Euergetes II the sanctuary leading out of the middle of the west wall of the upper court was enlarged by the addition of a third chamber, on the walls of which these heroes figured. Their special importance, at any rate in this period, was as patrons of healing and in this connection, Imhotep was identified by the Greeks in Egypt with their own god of medicine, Asklepios. Under their auspices Deir el Bahari seems to have become a regular place of resort for invalids, if we may judge from the numerous records which have been left by these visitors in the various parts of the precinct."

Deir el Bahari 12h. The tomb of Vizier Nespakashuty (Reign of Psamtek I, 664-610 B.C.) was not open for visitors on the day of this photographer's visit.

FREDERICK MONDERSON

Deir el Bahari 121. Close-up of sign for The Tomb of Vizier Nespakashuty (26th Dynasty 664-610 B.C).

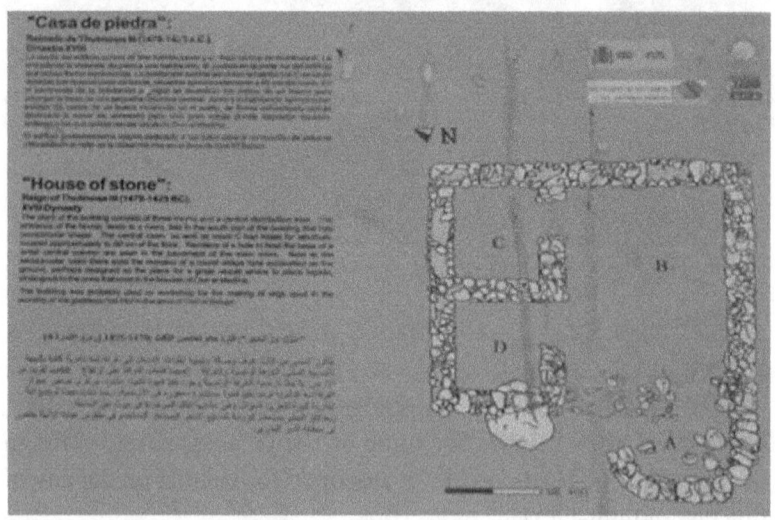

Deir el Bahari 12j. A "House of Stone" from the reign of Thutmose III, XVIIIth Dynasty (1479-1425 B.C.) in the Deir el Bahari vicinity.

HATSHEPSUT'S TEMPLE AT DEIR EL BAHARI

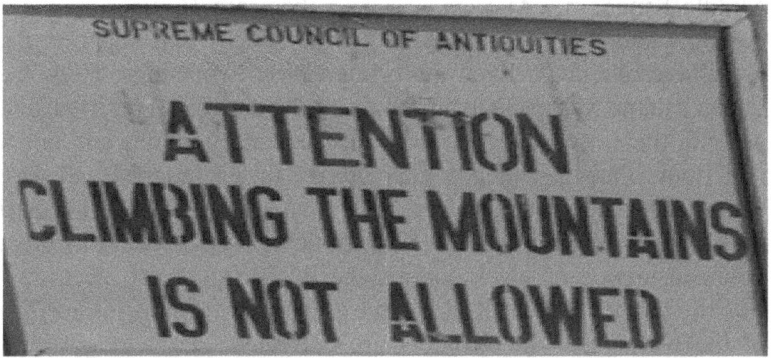

Deir el Bahari 12k. Sign indicating "Climbing the mountains is not allowed." Several photos taken from the mountain in this book were taken years ago when this fortunate "Bird's eye" vantage point to view of the temple was permitted in a trek from the direction of the Valley of the Kings.

Even further, Milne (1914: 96) continued: "The Upper Terrace of the temple backs-up against the cliffs on the west side in front, however, the east wall of the court is not on the edge of the terrace, but has a broad walk running along outside it, which was originally covered in as a colonnade. This colonnade seems to have been a convenient lounge for the ancient visitors who scratched their names on the outer face of the wall in many cases over the Egyptian reliefs."

Interestingly enough, Champollion, the linguist, who deciphered Hieroglyphics, was the first to name the peculiar columns he saw at Deir el Bahari as being "Proto-Doric." Speaking of Champollion's observations even though the temple was covered in debris in his time and having been visited by Pococke, Napoleon's savants before him and Wilkinson and Mariette after, Bratton (1968: 199) says Champollion thought: "The colonnades that he could see led to his theory that Greek art and architecture had their origin in Egypt. In both theories he anticipated the conclusions of archeologists a century later."

FREDERICK MONDERSON

These columns follow a pattern seen earlier at Beni Hasan in the Middle Kingdom. At Deir el Bahari there are 16 sides on these columns and there is no capital on the abacus that supports the architrave overhead. Even more interesting two things: First, the queen's name was hacked out and that of Thutmose III inserted; and second, there are descriptions of the dedicatory names and doors and floors that majestically characterize this wonderful and very beautiful piece of architecture. The "most splendid" Deir el Bahari is, according to Breasted II: "The temple of myriad years; its great doors fashioned of black copper, the inlaid figures of electrum." Equally too, it's called "Khikhet, the great seat of Amon, his horizon in the west," and all its doors are "of real cedar wrought with bronze." Breasted says even further regarding this wonderful place of mighty dignity: "The house of Amon, his enduring horizon of eternity" has floors that are "wrought with gold and silver, its beauty was like the horizon of heaven." In addition, he says, it is "A great shrine of ebony of Nubia" and "the stairs beneath it, high and wide" are made "of pure alabaster of Hatnub." It is therefore, "a palace of the God, wrought with gold and silver" and "it illuminated the faces (people) with its brightness."

As such then, in combination, these features make this temple the venerable yet majestically the most beautiful site that it is. Equally, it is also a photographer's paradise, particularly as it manifests a variety of colors depending upon the time when it is viewed or photographed. These then are reasons why Deir el Bahari is the fascination that it is.

References

Baedeker, Karl. *Egypt and the Sudan*: *Handbook for Travelers*. Leipzig: Karl Baedeker, Publisher, 1929.
Baikie, James. *Egyptian Antiquities in the Nile Valley*: *A Descriptive Handbook*. London: Methuen and Co., Ltd., 1932.
Bratton, Fred Gladstone. *A History of Egyptian Archaeology*. New York: Thomas Y. Crowell, Company, 1968.
Breasted, James Henry. *Ancient Records of Egypt*. 5 Vols. Chicago: University of Chicago Press, 1905-1907.

HATSHEPSUT'S TEMPLE AT DEIR EL BAHARI

Hall, H. R. *Handbook for Egypt and the Sudan*. London: Edward Stanford, (1907) 1910.
Milne, Joseph Grafton. "The Sanatorium at Deir el Bahari." *Journal of Egyptian Archaeology* VI (1914: 96-98).
Porter, Bertha and Rosalind B. Moss. *Topographical Bibliography of Ancient Egyptian Hieroglyphic Texts, Reliefs and Paintings: II Theban Temples*. Oxford: Griffith Institute, Ashmolean Museum, (1972) 1994.
West, John Anthony. *The Traveler's Keys to Ancient Egypt*. Wheaton, Illinois: Quest Books, 1995.
Wysocki, Z. "The Upper Court Colonnade of Hatshepsut's Temple at Deir el Bahari." *Journal of Egyptian Archaeology* 66 (1980: 54-69).

Deir el Bahari 12I. In the Sanctuary, the hands are Hatshepsut's offering the represented "Table of Offerings."

Illustration 16. The Queen receiving her troops.

Deir el Bahari 12m This time Hatshepsut offers to an enthroned Amon-Ra in the Temple's Sanctuary.

HATSHEPSUT'S TEMPLE AT DEIR EL BAHARI

6. QUEEN HATSHEPSUT-MA'AT-KA-RA OF THE 18TH DYNASTY.
By
Frederick Monderson

Queen Hatshepsut became Pharaoh of Upper and Lower Egypt and ruled from 1457 to 1437 B.C. She is considered a significant ruler of the early New Kingdom. This able woman became King of Egypt at a time when men dominated the life of governments in the ancient world. Therefore, such an act on her part was unthinkable. Bratton (1968: 196) expressed the view: "Hatshep might well be called the first great woman of history. She was the first woman to rule a nation unquestionably, maintaining the throne for 21 years against tough opposition." History informs; in the new political reality following expulsion of the Hyksos, Hatshepsut utilized beauty, intellect and daring together with alliances. In this, her loyal followers helped her gain power, which she exercised effectively.

Deir el Bahari 13. In front of the Temple, images of both tree trunks brought from Punt and planted here.

A lengthy reign enabled her to pursue extensive building and repair projects. Chief among these undertakings was her Mortuary Temple at Deir el-Bahari. This magnificent temple contains a pictorial representation of her expedition to Punt, perhaps the highlight of her reign. Moret (1912: 9) explained: "Although officially dedicated to Amon-Ra and his companion gods, Hathor and Anubis, the real divinity, whose glory the temple was intended to commemorate, was the Queen herself. The most elaborate picture and longest inscriptions are, therefore, devoted to an account of the life of the Queen, to the description of her birth, coronation, and the most memorable event of her reign - an expedition to the land of Punt, whence were brought the incense trees planted on the terraces. Other monuments, - two obelisks and a sanctuary in the great temple of Karnak, also an inscription in a chapel of Stabel-Antar, - have thrown some light upon the glorious reign of Queen Hatshopsitu, but Deir-el-Bahari is in relation to her what the temples of Abydos and Gournah are to Seti I; what the Ramesseum is to Rameses II, and Medinet-Habou to Rameses III – the place selected to commemorate the life and might of the Pharaoh. But in this case the Pharaoh of Deir-el-Bahari happens to be a woman."

Deir el Bahari 14. The Lower and Upper Colonnades against the mountain as a backdrop with the sky in the rear.

HATSHEPSUT'S TEMPLE AT DEIR EL BAHARI

Deir el Bahari 15. The author and photographer in the Second Court, at the Second Ramp leading to the Upper Colonnade and Terrace with the standing statues. Through the granite opening lies the Upper Court that houses its colonnade and the Sanctuary.

Of the first pair of obelisks she erected at Karnak, one still stands and the other lies beside the Sacred Lake. In fact, she erected four obelisks at Karnak, as depicted in a Deir el Bahari image, though the other two have since vanished. The one still standing was protected, ironically by a wall erected by Thutmose III, in his vengeance, to hide it from view and this protected it through his rampage and that of the later Amarna Revolution. Nevertheless, together, these structures tell us of her accomplishments. More importantly, organizational dynamics, building construction, respect for the gods and her father, as well as loyalty and firm reliance on key males in the Kingdom, are all significant factors that contributed to her successes.

Hatshepsut, *Ma'at-Ka-Ra*, was the daughter of Thutmose I. This King had four children. Steindorff and Seele (1971: 36) identified them as "two sons, Wadjmose and Amenmose, and two daughters Hatshepsut and Nefrubity." However, only one survived. Tuthmose I was the son of Amenhotep I and grandson of Ahmose I or Aahmes and his wife Nefertari. In Christian C. Bunsen's *Egypt's Place in Universal History III* (1854: 112-113) we find reference to the famous Queen Aahmose-Nefertari. Regarding this Nefertari, he confessed, "she is the illustrious heiress with whom he became acquainted when making researches about the 17th Dynasty – the Princess AAHMES NEFRU-ARI (the good, glorious woman). Her titles are: 'Royal wife, Mother, Daughter, Sister.' She was, consequently, the daughter of a Theban king, and, in fact, the daughter of an Ethiopian house, or one allied with Ethiopian blood. The historical representations describe her as black, unlike all the other Egyptian races. It is easy to understand that in those days Theban families intermarried with Ethiopian princes, for it was from the South only that they received any support and reserves during the struggle with the Shepherd Kings. It is probable that the Ethiopian ancestress, on the mother's side, received some provinces as her dowry; at all events, a portion of the country paid tribute to Amosis. Ne-fru-ari, then, was an heiress: she reigned in her right, and took the name 'Young Moon,' perhaps, in consequence of this inheritance; at any rate, it had reference to her, and was afterwards dropped. The monuments proved that no queen was ever held in such honor as this Aahmes. She is styled 'Divine Spouse of Ammon;' she enjoys the distinction of the barque of the Gods; and sits beside her son, Amenophis [Amenhotep] I, as if sharing equal rank with him, the reigning sovereign." Therefore, the young Queen Hatshepsut as descended from Nefertari was considered the only legitimate survivor of the old line of Theban Princes who expelled the Hyksos invaders from Egypt/Kemet/Tawi.

Significantly, she was also the great-granddaughter of Queen Aahmes-Nefertari. A portrait of the remarkable Queen Aahmes-Nefertari is displayed in the British Museum. This depiction shows the black complexioned beauty wearing the Queen-Mother Crown. Her dress, the fashion of the times, is probably the earliest representational use of the white, red and blue tricolor. In *Uncovering the African Past: The Van Sertima Papers* (2015) Runoko Rashidi displays another black image of Aahmes-Nefertari housed in the Berlin Museum. As such, to show affinity and kinship with this great ancestress of the Eighteenth Dynasty worked in Hatshepsut's favor and contributed to her successes.

HATSHEPSUT'S TEMPLE AT DEIR EL BAHARI

Deir el Bahari 16. Top and bottom close-up showing repaired pillars fronting round columns in the Southern Lower Colonnade

Deir el Bahari 17. Top and bottom close-up pillars fronting destroyed rear columns in the Northern Lower Colonnade. Above the Ramp in unfinished in its reconstruction by the Polish team.

FREDERICK MONDERSON

Now, the purpose of this part of the essay is to discuss aspects of the life and influence of this able female Pharaoh, who challenged male supremacy and left indelible impressions on the human, physical and historical landscape of Egypt. In addition, her architectural, diplomatic and foreign relations accomplishments as well as her associations with significant males in the kingdom will be examined. Further, an effective list of bibliographic references relating to the queen is supplied to encourage further research on her life and times. The life of her architect Senmut will also be included in the following part.

To acquire a clear understanding of Hatshepsut and her fortunes, a number of factors must be considered in the equation. The principal opponents to the throne did not have as illustrious a heritage as the Queen. In Breasted's *History of Egypt* (1909: 267) he writes: "Thutmose II was the son of a Princess Mutnefert; while the other, Thutmose III had been born to the king by an obscure concubine named Isis." In these respects, the queen had a natural right as successor to her father, Thutmose I. However, Egypt had a patrilineal system of succession (from father to son). Yet, this was nevertheless dependent on certain divine traits transmitted through the female line, that many, particularly Dr. Cheikh Anta Diop argue, was really matrilineal as the form of royal descent.

Deir el Bahari 17b. View from within the Southern Lower Colonnade with its outer pillars and destroyed inner Proto-Doric columns against a back wall.

HATSHEPSUT'S TEMPLE AT DEIR EL BAHARI

Deir el Bahari 17c. Panoramic view of the Upper court face of the Sanctuary area with the Mountain as a backdrop.

Deir el Bahari 17d. View from within the Northern Lower Colonnade with its outer pillars and inner Proto-Doric columns against a back wall as visitors mill around taking photographs.

Commenting on the issue of succession in the New Kingdom, Trigger, et-al (1989: 219) has argued it was "rapid and automatic, and practice reveals a general agreement that the heir in order of preference should be son of the chief queen, or of a lesser queen, or husband of a chief queen's daughter." This arrangement of male preference is what Hatshepsut challenged in choosing to rule. Still, in a way, though challenging the accepted order, she nevertheless reinforced the system of kingship by ruling as King, not Queen, of Egypt or ancient Kemet. In that she changed her name from Hatshepsitu to Hatshepsut and this is how we generally know her. However, there are many inscriptions of her name using female pronouns.

Illustration 17. Measuring the precious gum. (From Mariette's *Deir el Bahari*.)

All this, and notwithstanding, as Thutmose I grew older, he called together the great nobles of the land. The old king informed these defenders of the monarchical system, the lords of the court, that Hatshepsut would become ruler in his name. In this regard, Breasted (1909: 273) is quoted as saying: "Thutmose I told the assembled body 'Ye shall proclaim her word, ye shall be united at her command. He who shall do her homage shall live; he who shall speak evil in blasphemy of her majesty shall die.'"

Alexander Moret in *Kings and Gods of Egypt*, translated by Madame Moret (1912: 23-24) puts the king's words best in the statement: "This, my living daughter, Khnoumit-Amon Hatshepsitu, I place in my seat; I set her on my throne. Behold! She sits upon my throne; she makes her words heard in all parts of the palace; verily, she guides you. Hearken to her words and submit

HATSHEPSUT'S TEMPLE AT DEIR EL BAHARI

yourselves to her commands. He who adores her, behold! He shall live. He who speaks evil against Her Majesty, behold! He shall die. Let all those who hearken to her and with their whole hearts accept the name of Her Majesty come, even now, to proclaim her Queen beside me. Verily! This daughter of the gods is divine, and the gods fight for her and shed their fluid [of life] upon her neck every day, as was ordained by her father, the lord of the gods."

Deir el Bahari 18. A tourist mills around in the Southern Middle Colonnade with its double pillars and barrier.

Deir el Bahari 19. Illustrated pillars of the above image with a back wall on the Middle Colonnade.

FREDERICK MONDERSON

Deir el Bahari 19a and 19b. Southern Middle Colonnade houses the Punt Colonnade with the Upper Colonnade and the Upper Terrace above as visitors mill around enjoying the view; while climbing the reconstructed First and Second Ramps, the Lower Southern, Middle and Upper Colonnades reveal powerful features of the temple that showcase New Kingdom architectural magnificence and Senmut's genius.

In addition, Thutmose I was demanded that his daughter's 5 names be established as king. These, according to Breasted 06, II, 239) were as follows, as the inscription stated: "His majesty commanded that the ritual priests be brought to [proclaim] her great names that belonged to the assumption of the dignities of her royal crown and for insertion in (every) work and every seal of the Favorite of the Two Goddesses, who makes the circuit north of the wall, who clothes all the gods of the Favorite of the Two Goddesses. He has recognized the auspiciousness of the coronation on New Year's Day

HATSHEPSUT'S TEMPLE AT DEIR EL BAHARI

as the beginning of the peaceful years and of the spending of myriads (of years) of very many jubilees. They proclaim her royal names, for the god caused that it should be in their hearts to make her names according to the form with which he had made them before:

Her great name, Horus: [Wosretkew (*wsr. T-k'w*)], forever;
Her great name, Favorite of the Two Goddesses: 'Fresh in Years,' good goddess, mistress of offering;
Her great name, Golden Horus: 'Divine of diadems;'
Her Great name of King of Upper and Lower Egypt: 'Makere, who liveth forever.' It is her real name which the god made beforehand."
The fifth name, Son of Ra, was the name given at her birth, Hatshepsut.

Still, as if adding more ammunition to her cause, an inscription on the Eighth Pylon at Karnak which Breasted (1906, II, 245) explained was concocted by the Queen herself, tells how Thutmose I made a plea to Amon on his daughter's behalf. Breasted recounts the following address to show the special nature of his request that was ground-breaking in seeking the god's blessing on a female. Thutmose stated: "I come to thee, lord of Gods; I do obeisance [before] thee, in return for this that [thou hast put] the Black and Red Land under (the dominion of) my daughter, the King of Upper and Lower Egypt, Makere (Hatshepsut), who lives forever, just as thou didst put (it) under (the dominion of) my majesty .... Thou hast given to me the kingdom of every land in the presence of the Two Lands, exalting my beauty while I was a youth .... [the Black land] and the Red Land are under my dominion. I am satisfied with victories, thou hast placed every rebellious land under my sandals which thy serpent-diadem has bound, bearing their gifts; thou hast strengthened the fear [of me] their limbs tremble, I have seized them in victory according to thy command; they are made my subjects; [they come to me] doing obeisance, and all countries with bowed head. Tribute --- --- ..... the heart of my majesty is glad because of her ---- [the petition] concerning my daughter Wosretkew, King of Upper and Lower Egypt, of whom thou hast

desired, that she be associated with [thee] [that] thou mightest assign [this] land [to] her grasp. Make her prosperous as King mayest thou [grant] for
me the prayer of the first time, my petition concerning [my] beloved (fem.) ---- ... under her majesty (fem.)"

Yet, the old King knew the opposition and intrigues she would face. After this elevated recognition she toured the land with her father where she learned administrative procedures, and duties and responsibilities of the Pharaoh. The respect she felt for Thutmose I became enshrined in her architectural projects. Such action on her part caused the people to love her. As a result, Hatshepsut became an able administrator who repaired the temples left in disarray, created civil projects, encouraged learning and creativity, promoted travel to intra-Egypt historic monuments, and pursued trade relations with neighboring states.

Hatshepsut's apprenticeship with her father served her well. The young Queen continued his aggressive foreign policy. She pacified Nubia and established contact with the lands north of Egypt. As was customary, she married Thutmose II, the expected heir, and had a girl child by him. Soon he died. At that time women could only legitimize the heir or pharaoh, but not rule in their stead. Yet, she became co-regent with her half-brother Thutmose III, some say the son of Thutmose II, thus her step-son. However, her party of influential and powerful followers soon thrust him aside and she assumed complete control over Egypt. With this, Bratton (1968: 196-97) notes, she took the title: "Chief Spouse of Amon, the Mighty One, the Lord of East and West, the Good Goddess, the Pious Lady, the Beautiful Falcon in her Risings, the King of Upper and Lower Egypt, the Daughter of Ra, Khnumit-Amon-Hatshepsut." Nobles and other well-wishers soon addressed the beautiful ruler as *Her Majesty Himself*, Queen Hatshepsut.

J.A. Rogers has supplied a vivid but brief biography of Hatshepsut. In his account (I, 1972: 47) we are told: "She donned male garb, changed her name from Hatshepsitu to Hatshepsut, its male

HATSHEPSUT'S TEMPLE AT DEIR EL BAHARI

equivalent, and announced that she was of Divine Birth. Her father, she claimed was not Thutmose I, but the great God Amen himself. The latter appeared to her mother in a flood of light and perfume." These events became a significant turning point in her career. It influenced all future relationships and provided a sort of justification for her efforts to placate the gods, all aided by a party of influential and loyal individuals.

Deir el Bahari 20. More illustrated pillars in two rows in the northern section of the Middle Colonnade.

Deir el Bahari 20a. Northern section of the Lower and Middle Colonnades front the Upper Colonnade and Terrace as visitors climb the Second Ramp towards the Granite doorway entering the Upper Court with the Sanctuary against the mountain's back wall.

FREDERICK MONDERSON

Deir el Bahari 20b. Visitors come and go in the Middle Court to view the "Birth Colonnade" (left) and the Anubis Shrine (right) part of the Northern Middle Colonnade, while others view statues and columns in the Upper Terrace.

Deir el Bahari 20c. To the left pillars front the "Birth Colonnade" beside the Shrine of Anubis with Proto-Doric columns in front and rear.

HATSHEPSUT'S TEMPLE AT DEIR EL BAHARI

Deir el Bahari 20d. The Anubis Shrine is center right beside first columns of the Northern Colonnade. Look closely there you can see the joints of the beams that join in the center of the column's abacus spanning the void to create the architrave, especially in the Anubis Shrine. To the right are first columns of the Northern Colonnade.

Deir el Bahari 20e. The Shrine of Anubis with Proto-Doric columns in front and rear. Off to the right, columns of the Northern Colonnade, with the three rooms in rear and the mountain as a backdrop.

FREDERICK MONDERSON

Deir el Bahari 20f. A closer view of the "True Northern Colonnade" with its 15 columns and unfinished architrave all before the three small rooms at the rear thought to be places for worship of deities of the temple. Look for the architrave beam that centers on the flat abacus atop the Proto-Doric columns.

Deir el Bahari 21. Second Security post before the First Court, and First Ramp with Lower, Middle and Upper Colonnades visible.

Her party of principal backers comprised a close and powerful group of nobles who held key administrative positions in the state. The closest and most favored was Senmut, her architect, who built

HATSHEPSUT'S TEMPLE AT DEIR EL BAHARI

the Deir el-Bahari Temple. He was the Tutor of her daughter Princess Nefru-Re, a firm supporter, who held many important positions of power. She made him Minister of Finance, Minister of Works, Hereditary Prince and Count, Conductor of Festivals, Overseer of the Garden of Amun, and so on. Some scholars believe, Kamil (1980: 76) writes he may have held "no fewer than 40 titles" altogether. Even more so, others think he was intimate with her due to the closeness of their relationship. One particular writer, Hobson (1987: 183) bases this view on a scene at Deir el-Bahari and suggests: "In the center of the second terrace, enter the inner rooms used for the mortuary offerings. In two small dark 'cupboards,' use a torch on the side walls to see a small carved image of a man with his name, Senmut, in hieroglyphs; he was Hatshepsut's chief advisor and treasurer, and some say, her lover."

The other members of his party who supported the Queen were Nehsi, the Chancellor and leader of the expedition to Punt. His efforts immortalized her diplomatically in establishing trade and other familial relations with inner Africa. Thutiy and Thutnofre were treasurers of the North and South Kingdoms. Puyemre was the Second Prophet of Amun, Lord of Thebes. Hapu-Seneb was Vizier or Prime Minister, the Chief Administrative Officer in the land. Ineby was her Viceroy to Nubia, an important post in Egypto-other-African states' affairs. Dewaemhen was the First Herald and Tetyenre was a Scribe. These individuals supported her and tied their fortunes to hers. When she was succeeded or deposed by Thutmose III, after a reign of nearly two decades, his wrath fell upon them for delaying his rise or ascension to the Throne of Egypt/Kemet. Thutmose III later destroyed or defaced the Queen's name and monuments and those of many of her many followers, particularly the tomb of Senmut in the Second Court of the Deir el Bahari Precinct. Here he constructed this tomb in addition to his first tomb at Sheikh Abd el Kurneh.

Deir el Bahari 22. View from the Second Ramp of the Middle Colonnade showing round columns in rear fronted by square pillars on the south side of the Lower Colonnade. The same appears on the north side, though these are badly destroyed.

Deir el Bahari 22a. Classic view of the reconstructed Second Ramp leading to the Upper Terrace.

HATSHEPSUT'S TEMPLE AT DEIR EL BAHARI

Deir el Bahari 23. *Suten Bat* title above Ra designation in cartouche, probably belonging to Thutmose III, Men-Kheppe-Ra.

FREDERICK MONDERSON

Some scholars and commentators tend to decry the early 18th Dynasty assertiveness as a time, according to Lesko (1967: 114) of "vainglory" as it related to Senmut, the Queen's favorite. This may be because the noble boasted of his numerous titles and the power he wielded. The Queen, on the other hand, as principal figure in the kingdom, was no less prolific in lofty descriptions of her divine person. She is shown styling herself, Steindorff and Seele (1971: 41) says as "exceedingly good to look upon, with the form and spirit of a god, a beautiful maiden, fresh, serene of nature, altogether divine."

In the tombs prepared for her, equally high sounding descriptions of the queen were made such as that she was "*The hereditary princess, great in favor and grace, mistress of all lands, king's daughter, king's sister, wife of the god, great wife of the king, lady of the two lands, Hatshepsut.*" This was before she assumed her more exalted titles "*Horus rich-in-kas, Two Goddesses, green-in-years, Horus-of-Gold, divine-of-appearances, King of Upper and Lower Egypt, Makare, daughter of Re, United-to-Amen, Hatshepsuit.*"

In her youthful and serene beauty, as indicated, when appointed co-Regent with her father she journeyed with him on inspections around the country. On these occasions, Steindorff and Seele's *When Egypt Ruled the East* (1942, 1957: 41) add further, all the gods "came to her." These divinities included: "Hathor of Thebes, Wadjet of Buto, Amun, Lord of Karnak, Amun of Heliopolis, Montu [the god of war] Lord of Thebes, in fact, all the gods of Upper and Lower Egypt promising her protection and good fortune for her reign if she would in future years dedicate herself to the gods and the temples." Maybe, this promise was the driving force behind Hatshepsut's grand strategy to legitimize her rule of Egypt. The assertive Ma'at-Ka-Ra erected temples, repaired and restored sanctuaries and re-established cult worship in many centers. She also undertook social reform projects to cause the people to disregard the fact she was a woman. The female Pharaoh entrusted the government of the state to able administrators. Together, they helped to maintain the high level of accomplishments Egypt had experienced from the start of the XVIIIth Dynasty. With the

HATSHEPSUT'S TEMPLE AT DEIR EL BAHARI

exception of the Nubian expedition, militarily her reign was relatively calm, a necessity for a nation to create social infrastructure designed to improve the lot of its people. She is credited with pursuing trade and diplomatic relations with her cousins to the south of Egypt, in the land of Punt.

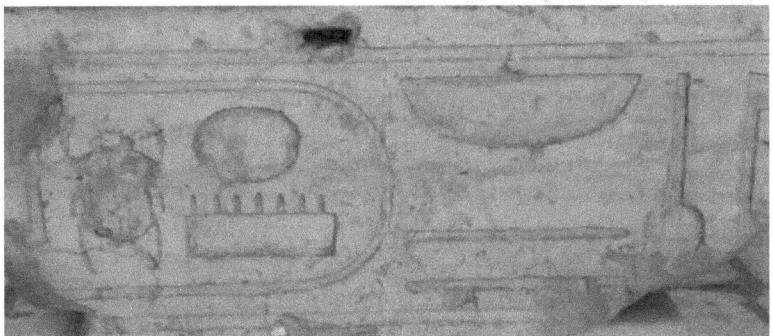

Deir el Bahari 24. Part of *Suten Bat* title of Tuthmose III, *Men Khepper Ra*.

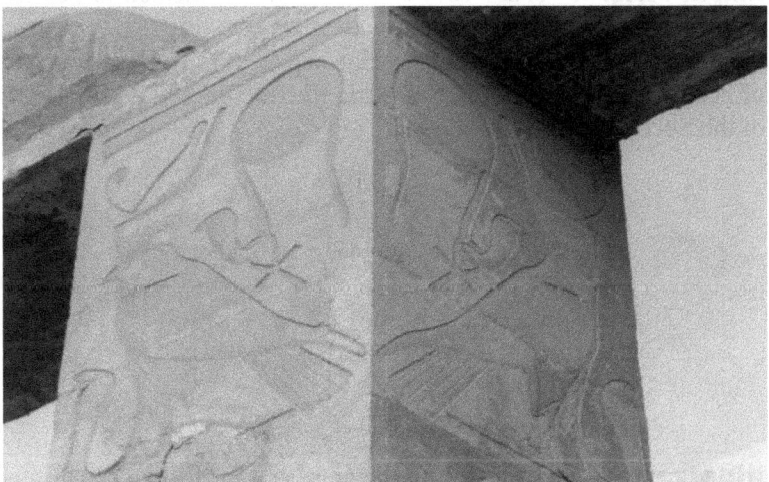

Deir el Bahari 25. Square pillar at the Hathor Shrine depicting hawk wearing the Double Crown with Disk and swinging uraeus holding ankh overhead and uraeus below.

FREDERICK MONDERSON

Economic prosperity attended the land during her reign since there was minimal expenditure for military ventures. The expedition to Punt was indeed a successful economic and diplomatic enterprise. Even more so, Aldred (1987: 149) praises it as "the first known example of an anthropological study of an alien culture, with its record of flora and fauna of the region, the human types, their physique, dress and habitations."

Hatshepsut's reign added more creative features, particularly the encouragement of intellectual development. Elsewhere, Aldred (1980: 150) points out: "Graffiti disclose that the Step-Pyramid of Djoser, besides other famous monuments, was being visited by learned scribes as early as the reign of Amenophis I, and this study was increased with intensity during the reign of Hatshepsut." This revelation therefore credits her with the cultivation of learning in diverse branches of knowledge adding to her stature of being *avant-garde* in architectural, theological and philosophical creativity. In addition, at Beni Hasan in Middle Egypt, Hatshepsut erected a rock-cut chapel, the ancient Greeks called *Speos Artemidos*. This small temple, Murnane (1983: 187) explained, was dedicated to Pakhet, "She who scratches," a lion-goddess of the district. Wilson mentions inscriptions also left by Hatshepsut at Beni Hasan, as part of her efforts of restoration following the rule of the Hyksos Kings of the Second Intermediate Period.

Illustration 18. Heralding the approach of the Queen. Either the government has a factory that makes "uniform wigs" for these Nubians and elsewhere, or its their real hair!

HATSHEPSUT'S TEMPLE AT DEIR EL BAHARI

The Queen has here preserved a most important historical reference to the rule of the Hyksos in Egypt. Wilson (1959: 160) quotes her as saying: "I have restored that which had been ruined. I have raised up (again) that which had formerly gone to pieces, since the Asiatics were in the midst of Avaris of the Delta, and vagabonds were in their midst, overthrowing what had been made, for they ruled without Re and he did not act by divine command down to (the reign of) my majesty. I have made distant those whom the gods abominate, and earth has carried off their foot (prints)."

This significant document pertains to the time of Hyksos rule the Queen has preserved for us. The only other inscription for that period comes from the Nineteenth Dynasty. More popular, it tells the famous story of the Hyksos King Apophis' arrogant letter to Thebans complaining their Hippos, wading in the Nile, were disturbing his sleep at nights, though hundreds of miles to the north. So disturbing was this provocative statement that the Theban princes galvanized their military effort and began the revolutionary war that ended with the expulsion of the Hyksos and formation of the 18th Dynasty and New Kingdom, under Aahmose I.

Deir el Bahari 26. Just before the First Ramp, square pillars front round columns of the southern half of the Lower Colonnade with the Second Ramp and Middle and Upper Colonnades partially visible. Notice the opening to the Upper Court to the top right

FREDERICK MONDERSON

Deir el Bahari 27 and 28. Northern half of the Middle Colonnade showing the rear wall and the rear row of columns (left); and again, Northern half of the Middle Colonnade showing the front and rear row of pillars.

There are several other projects Hatshepsut initiated. In addition to the Sinai mines, which she exploited from the fifth year of her reign, several buildings and repair projects were also undertaken. She built a temple at Bhutan in Nubia, later enlarged by Thutmose III. Here a Middle Kingdom fortress stood and commercial enterprise was cultivated with interior Africa. Bratton (1968: 277) believes, "the unusual feature of this temple is the colonnade which has alternating square pillars and round columns. The inner courts are decorated with polychrome reliefs and many of the paintings have retained their original color." This pillar and column alternation found its greatest success at *Desheru Deshret*, the "Holy of Holies," "Deir el Bahari" or the "Northern Monastery," so named by Egyptian Christians in the Seventh Century of our era.

Hatshepsut built the small chapel in the northwest corner of the Court of Rameses II at the Luxor Temple of Amenhotep III. Just opposite the Abu Haggag Mosque, the small chapel that's wrongfully credited to Tuthmose III was dedicated to the Theban

HATSHEPSUT'S TEMPLE AT DEIR EL BAHARI

Triad of Amun, Mut and Khonsu. In his Ramessean Front Court, Rameses II did repairs and left his name there. The queen also built a Festival Temple at Medinet Habu, a site later glorified by Rameses III's Mortuary Temple. She erected a shrine at Karnak for the Sacred Bark. She constructed the Eight Pylon at Karnak, linking that temple with the temple of Mut to the south. This edifice has a strange history.

The Eighth Pylon, built by Hatshepsut, is considered one of the oldest structures at Karnak Temple. Mokhtar (ND: 38) tells: "Thutmose III wiped out the name of Hatshepsut to take revenge on her for depriving him of the throne when he was young and instead wrote his name. Then came Akhenaton; he wiped out the name of the God Amon-Ra and inscribed the name of Aton, God of the Sun. Thereafter, came Seti I of the XIX Dynasty: he wiped out the name of Akhenaton and the God Aton and replaced them with his name and the name of the God Amon."

Still, Hatshepsut's most overwhelming project at Karnak was the erection of two rose granite obelisks, quarried at Aswan, by her architect Senmut in the fifteenth year of her reign. This, like all her major architectural undertakings were in honor of Amun, underscoring her deep religiosity and remembering the divinities' admonition when they "came to her." Bratton (1968: 198) says the Queen states: "I sat in the Palace. I remembered him who fashioned me; my heart led me to make for him two obelisks of electrum, whose points mingled with heaven."

It took Senmut seven months to quarry, transport and erect them in the "colonnaded Hall of the Karnak Temple" Bratton (1968: 198) noted: "where Tuthmose III had been named king by the Amon oracle. Senmut had the roof of the temple removed in order to accommodate the obelisk. The one in place stands 97 1/2 feet high, contains one hundred and eighty cubic yards of granite and weighs 350 tons." Steindorff and Seele (1971: 43) tells, "the points of the obelisk were covered with gold in order that they might be seen on both sides of the river, and their rays inundated the two lands whenever the sun rose between them, just as it appears in the horizon of heaven."

Illustration 19 and 20. Throne-Chair of Queen Hatasu. (From a photograph of the original in the British Museum) (left); and Little Cabinet of Hatasu containing the "Tooth" used to finally identify the Queen's mummy.

In fact, Hatshepsut actually erected four obelisks at Karnak, but two have vanished over the years, while the apex of one lies one hundred feet away, in front of the "Coca Cola Temple" beside the Sacred Lake. Still, there were other structures at Karnak that attest to her work in praise of the gods. On the other side of the "Holy of Holies," Sanctuary, Steindorff and Seele (1971: 165) explain, "is a group of rooms built and decorated by Queen Hatshepsut." Here evidence of Thutmose III's animosity depicts her images systematically defaced. In addition, Steindorff and Seele (1971: 166) continued, regarding the location behind the Sanctuary: "East of the festival hall and backing the outer stone enclosure wall of the main temple precinct is a somewhat mysterious sanctuary which appears to have been begun by Hatshepsut and completed by Tuthmose III. It faces toward the east; its chief features were a chapel containing the seated figures of the royal couple, the whole carved from a single gigantic block of alabaster, a row of six Osiride or jubilee statues of the king, and, flanking the north and south ends of the structure, a pair of red granite obelisks (now fallen) of the queen."

HATSHEPSUT'S TEMPLE AT DEIR EL BAHARI

The Lady was extremely busy even as she encouraged ritual worship of the gods. Thus, in her orchestrated many respects, people only saw her good works, respect for her people, the land and the gods. These actions were how she legitimized her reign and further consolidated her power base. Following Thutmose II's death and with Thutmose III cast aside, with herself firmly in charge, he took the title that reflected her supremacy in the kingdom. She now became: "King of the North and South, Ka-Ma-Ra, the Horus of Gold; Bestower of Years; Ruler of All Lands; Vivifier of Hearts; Chief Spouse of Amen; the Mighty One."

In that busyness, J.A. Wilson in *The Culture of Ancient Egypt* (1951, 1971: 174) yet compared her with Thutmose who succeeded to the throne and the view that distinguished them. "The reigns of Hat-shepsut and of Thut-mose III contrast strongly in the activities of the state. She records no military campaigns or conquests; he became the great conqueror and organizer of empire. Her pride was in the internal development of Egypt and in commercial enterprise; his pride was in the external expansion of Egypt and in military enterprise. This was a conflict between the older concept of the Egyptian state, an isolated and superior culture, which needed to express no major concern about other countries because no other country presented an important challenge to Egypt, and the new concept of the Egyptian state, a culture which felt obliged to assert its superiority by capturing and holding foreign territory. Through the time of Hat-shepsut, the foreign contacts had been exploited through commercial and cultural penetration, to the material advantage of both parties. Thut-mose III was to introduce a formal and consistent policy of military and political imperialism, in order to gain security at home by pushing Egypt's effective frontier far beyond her geographic borders and in order to control foreign commerce by her own army and navy. The formal introduction of imperialism ended Egypt's formal insolation, had a profound effect upon Egyptian psychology, and ultimately brought the characteristic Egyptian culture to an end."

FREDERICK MONDERSON

The contrast, notwithstanding, the people, of her ancient Nile Valley country, Kemet, saw only her good works, respect for the people, the land and the gods. These actions were how she legitimized her reign and further consolidated her power base. Now firmly in charge, she took the title that reflected her supremacy in the kingdom. She now became: "King of the North and South, Ka-Ma-Ra; the Horus of Gold; Bestower of Years; Ruler of All Lands; Vivifier of Hearts; Chief Spouse of Amen; the Mighty One."

However, Hatshepsut's greatest and seemingly most lasting achievement was the construction of Deir el-Bahari, which Steindorff and Seele (1970: 170) reported was styled "Splendid are the Splendors of Amon." Breasted recounts its description as "a great shrine of ebony of Nubia; the stairs beneath it, high and wide, of pure alabaster of Hat Nub." Even further, it's been called: "A palace of the god, wrought with gold and silver, it illuminated the faces (of people) with its brightness."

Located at Thebes, in Upper Egypt, this wonderful structure was patterned after the nearby Temple of Mentuhotep II, built 500 years earlier, during the Middle Kingdom. Her magnificent Mortuary Temple against the western cliffs was unique. Bratton (1968: 194) believed, the "appeal of this structure derives from beauty of line, unity and coherence rather than massiveness." He stated: "To build this temple at the base of a mountainous wall of rock required nothing short of genius, for the magnificent background of the awesome cliffs could easily have been the architect's downfall. Such a backdrop could well have dwarfed the temple into insignificance and the attempt to compete with the beautiful natural setting was an invitation to disaster. The Giza pyramids compel our admiration because of their contrast to the flat desert, stretching endlessly at their base. But at Deir el Bahari the builder saw that pylons, obelisks, and gigantic papyrus columns could only have the effect of a dog barking at a lion. He wisely avoided any attempt at height and erected a structure which emphasized horizontal lines, knowing that only such an arrangement could survive on the background of the overwhelming cliff."

HATSHEPSUT'S TEMPLE AT DEIR EL BAHARI

This temple, greater than her ancestor Mentuhotep's, the tunnel and a tomb in the Valley of the Kings as opposed to one in the Valley of the Queens, are some of the factors that maligned her name with Thutmose III and other critical Pharaohs, particularly the Ramessides.

Deir el Bahari 28a. – You decide why the Cobra is here!

Deir el Bahari 29. View of the heads of two standing Osiride Figures of the Queen on the Upper Colonnade or Upper Terrace. Here, pillars front Proto-Doric columns.

FREDERICK MONDERSON

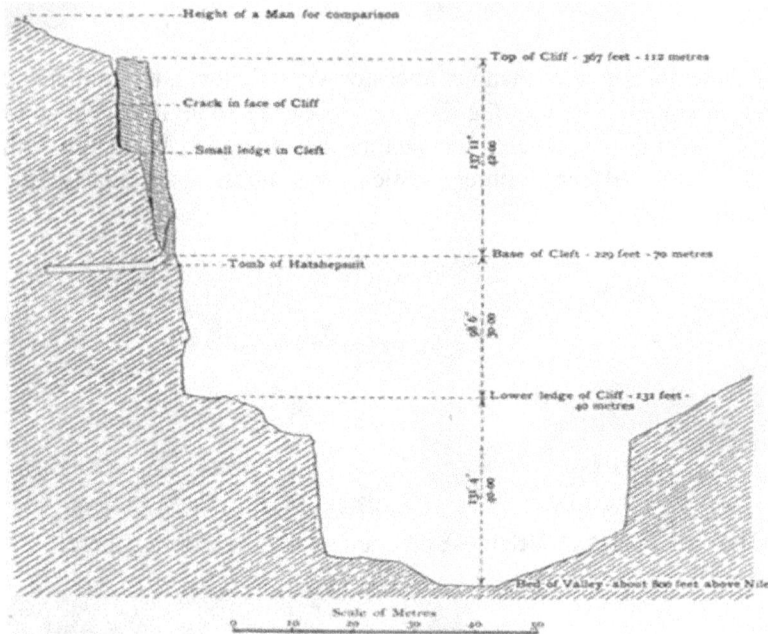

Illustration 21. The gorge chosen for the first tomb of Hatshepsut.

The tomb had several peculiarities, being one of the earliest 18th Dynasty, New Kingdom, tombs in the Valley, following Thutmose I's decision to be buried here as opposed to the plains where earlier kings were interred. In "A Tomb Prepared for Queen Hatshepsut and Other Recent Discoveries at Thebes" Howard Carter (*Journal of Egyptian Archaeology* 4, 1917: 107-118) has written: "The design of the tomb is as follows. A flight of steps (A) descends to an entrance doorway at the bottom of the cleft. The doorway opens directly into a descending gallery some 17 meters long and averaging 2.20 meters in height (B). At the end of this first gallery, on the right hand, is a small antechamber or portcullis chamber (C), whence a steep gallery (D) descends, 5.30 meters in length. This leads directly into the sepulchral hall (E), a rectangular room measuring 5.40 x 5.30 meters and 3 meters in height. Cut in the floor of the sepulchral hall on the side opposite to the doorway is a small steep passage (F) descending into an incomplete chamber (G),

HATSHEPSUT'S TEMPLE AT DEIR EL BAHARI

which appears to be the commencement of the crypt. Over the mouth of the descending passage (F) rests the magnificent sarcophagus of yellow crystalline sandstone, as though on its way to its final resting-place, which was doubtless never completed crypt .... There were no traces that the tomb had ever contained a burial, the only objects that were found besides the sarcophagus and its lid being two broken necks of pottery jars such as were used by workmen."

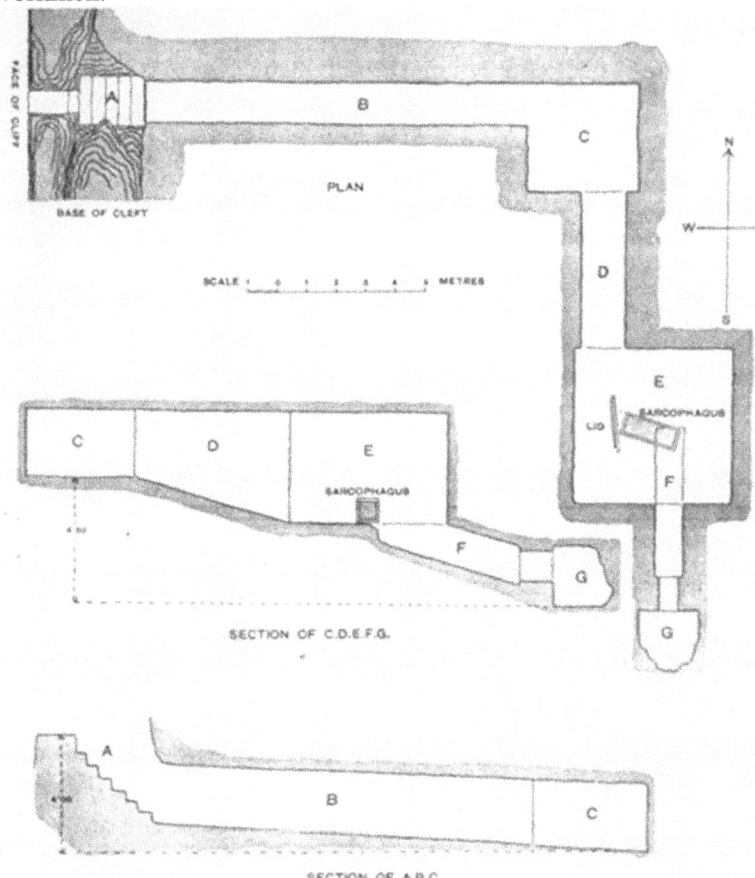

Illustration 22. Plan of the "first" Tomb of Hatshepsut.

FREDERICK MONDERSON

Texts on the sarcophagus give the queen's name as *"the hereditary princess, great in favor and grace, mistress of all lands, king's daughter, king's sister, wife of the god, great wife of the king, land of the two lands, Hatshepsut"* and assuming full control of the state this was changed to the loftier title already stated.

This tomb itself in the Valley of the Kings rather than her earlier one in the Valley of the Queens was discovered in 1903 by Howard Carter working on behalf of Theodore Davis. Its beautiful sarcophagus, according to Carter measured 1.99 meters in length, 0.73 meters in breadth, and 0.17 meters in thickness. Carved upon the upper surface is a cartouche enclosing a figure of the goddess Nut facing towards the left with her arms upraised. In front of the goddess is a vertical legend reading: *"Recitation. The king's daughter, wife of the god, great wife of the king, lady of the two lands Hatshepsuit (Hatshepsut), she says: O my mother Nut, stretch thyself over me, that thou mayst place me among the stars imperishable that are in thee, and that I may not die."*

In a Horizontal band, the Sarcophagus' Head-end has the following inscription: *"Recitation. O wife of the god, great wife of the king, Hatshepsuit, I am Isis, I am Nephthys.*

Vertical columns Recitation reads: *"O king's daughter, Hatshepsuit, we are come that we may raise thee, that they heart may live."*

"Recitation. O king's sister, Hatshepsuit, we embrace thy flesh, we command thy limbs to live, and thou diest not."

On the Foot-end. Horizontal band, we find: *"Recitation. O king's daughter, king sister, wife of the god, great wife of the king, Hatshepsuit. I am thy sister Isis."*

Two vertical columns read: *"Recitation. O wife of the god Hatshepsuit, I have come rejoicing through love of thee."* Again, *"Recitation. O king's sister, Hatshepsuit, I have come that I may take hold of thee."*

HATSHEPSUT'S TEMPLE AT DEIR EL BAHARI

On the *Left* side, Horizontal Band, the inscription reads: *"Recitation by Geb. O wife of the god, great wife of the king, Hatshepsuit, raise thee to thy mother Nut, that she may take hold of thee and embrace thee. O king's sister, Hatshepsuit, I stand up as one who tendeth thee. O wife of the god, Hatshepsuit, thy heart swelleth, Horus has rescued thee."*

In addition, there are four vertical columns that read as follows:

1. *Honored before Imseti, the king's wife, Hatshepsuit, justified before Osiris."*

2. *Honored before Thoth, the great wife of the king, Hatshepsuit, justified."*

3. *Honored before Anubis in front of the divine booth, the wife of the god, Hatshepsuit, justified."*

4. *Honored before Dua-mutef, the lady of the two lands, Hatshepsut, justified before Osiris.*

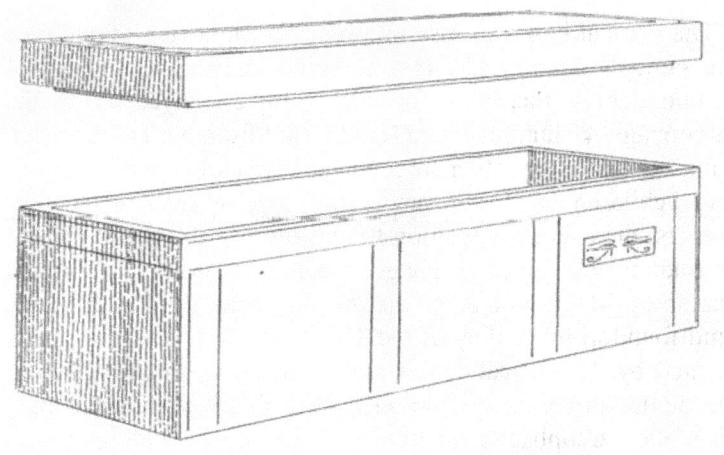

Illustration 23. Sarcophagus of Hatshepsut.

FREDERICK MONDERSON

On the RIGHT SIDE, a Horizontal band reads. *"Recitation by Nut. I have examined the hereditary princess, great in favor and grace, mistress of all lands, king's daughter, king's sister, wife of the god, great wife of the king, Hatshepsuit, living. Mayst thou not perish, I destroy thy disability wife of the god, lady of the two lands, Hatshepsuit, living. Thoth hath given the gods to thee."*

Here four vertical lines read:

1. Honored before Kebhsenuf, the king's sister, Hatshepsuit, justified before Osiris.

2. *"Honored before Anubis Imi-ut, the wife of the god, Hatshepsuit, justified."*

2. *"Honored before Horus who is in the sky, the wife of the god, Hatshepsuit, justified."*

4. *"Honored before Hapy, the wife of the god, Hatshepsuit, justified before Osiris."*

["The vertical bands of inscription on the right and left sides of the sarcophagus describe Hatshepsuit as under the tutelage of certain deities, the same formula being employed as on the sarcophagi of Thutmosi I and Hatshepsuit from the Tombs of the Kings and on many other sarcophagi, both earlier and later. The four "children of Horus" are named, one at each of the four corners; their relative position to one another and to the general orientation of the sarcophagus seems to vary in different examples. Mr. Carter notes that on the sarcophagi of the same kind found in the Valley of the Tombs of the Kings, the panels formed by the vertical columns of inscription contain figures of the deities mentioned in these; clearly this was intended here also, the sarcophagus having been abandoned before it was complete. Mr. Carter suggests this conclusion by remarking that the sarcophagus has not been painted as are the similar

HATSHEPSUT'S TEMPLE AT DEIR EL BAHARI

sarcophagi from the Tombs of the Kings, and that some of the guiding lines for the sculptor are still visible.]"

"The tomb was discovered full of rubbish from its mouth to its very end and from floor to ceiling, this rubbish having poured into it in torrents from the mountain above. When I wrested it from the plundering Arabs, I found that they had burrowed into it like rabbits, as far as the sepulchral hall. The burrow made by them was some twenty-nine meters long and would allow but one man to pass at a time and then only by creeping upon his stomach. They had widened and deepened the burrows for further operations – which never eventuated! I found that they had crept down a crack extending half-way down the cleft, and there from a small ledge in the rocks they had lowered themselves by a rope to the then hidden entrance of the tomb at the bottom of the cleft: a dangerous performance, but one which I myself had to imitate, though with better tackle, this being the only means of first reaching the opening so as to establish easier and safer methods of access from below. This I did eventually by erecting sheers of timber of adequate strength over the mouth of the tomb and also a projecting stage at the base of the cleft; these enabled us to haul ourselves up and down from below. For anyone who suffers from vertigo it certainly was not pleasant, and though I soon overcame the sensation of the ascent I was obliged to descend in a net. The operations, inclusive of the transport of the necessary materials to the spot, the fixing of the scaffolding, and the clearing of the tomb from end to end, took twenty days, the work continuing both day and night with relays of workmen for the night shifts.

Significantly, the **Abydos Tablet** was not kind to Hatshepsut's name and memory. The **Abydos Temple** was begun by Seti I and completed by his son, Rameses II. The **Corridor of Kings**, an east wing appendage of the Abydos Temple contains a list of 76 cartouches of Kings of Egypt from Menes to Seti I. Five of the cartouches are blank due to some perceived transgression of the Kingship of Egypt/Kemet, by their

FREDERICK MONDERSON

owners. The rulers whose cartouches are blank include Hatshepsut and Akhenaton, the XVIIIth Dynasty religious reformer, together with his immediate successors, Smenkare, Tutankhamon and Aye. While these latter Pharaohs were proscribed for their association with the Amarna Revolution against Amun, King of the Gods, Hatshepsut's sin was daring to rule as Pharaoh, dressing as a man, wearing a false beard, planning to construct the tunnel and building the tomb in the Valley of the Kings. She also built a temple greater than her ancestor Mentuhotep.

Gaston Maspero, a Frenchman in charge of the Cairo Museum at the end of the Nineteenth Century, is responsible for setting up many of the display cards of the exhibit. Some of his pronouncements on several of the displays are extremely controversial. One such statement was a description of Maherpra, a 19th Dynasty nobleman. Based on his Black features represented on the *Maherpra Papyrus*, Maspero thought him "Negroid but not Negro." Nevertheless, this scholar did extensive excavation and writing on the subject of ancient Egyptian culture. He provided interesting information on Egyptian temple construction.

Certain ceremonies were practiced when building a temple. At the start of construction of a new temple or rebuilding of an old one, it was customary, says Maspero (1926: 54-55) for builders to: "place deposits under the foundation consisting of small squares of the building materials and samples of the tools employed. Also, a number of amulets, which were probably intended to secure by magic the safety of the temple. Next, the name of the royal founder was inscribed on the spot. Tools and other objects of the foundation deposits were placed in a layer of clean sand." Maspero (1926: 55) says further: "Among the glazed objects found in this deposit were scarabs, plaques, models of offerings, besides many beads. The metal objects include adze, knife, axe-head, hoes, and chisels, made in thin sheet copper. There were also jars and cups, an ebony clamp, and a model corn-grinder."

HATSHEPSUT'S TEMPLE AT DEIR EL BAHARI

At Deir el-Bahari, models of workmen's tools were unearthed, including "wooden centerings used in brick vaulting." The excavators found blue ink scarabs with Hatshepsut's cartouche. Archaeologists also found, at the western entrance of the building, as Maspero (1926: 55-56) explained: "... evidence of a ceremony customary at the foundation of the temple. An animal was slain and the flesh laid on a floor of clean sand over which the blood was allowed to drip; vessels containing unguents and wine were smashed and their contents, together with grains of corn, were poured into the cache in addition to the offering of flesh, tools and blood."

Deir el Bahari 29a. Wall and decoration among the many features of the temple.

FREDERICK MONDERSON

Deir el Bahari 30. Close-up of an end Osiride Figure of the Queen wearing the White Crown, with beard and holding whip and flail.

HATSHEPSUT'S TEMPLE AT DEIR EL BAHARI

Deir el Bahari 31. Hathor Head figure wearing female face, cow's ears and with cascading braids of hair.

FREDERICK MONDERSON

The ground plan of the temple showed several innovative features. These designs made it a magnificent work of architecture that endured through the years. Oriented slightly southeast to northwest, it had an uncompleted Valley Temple at the river's edge. In this regard, Haag (1987: 240) has written: "From this temple ran a promenade lined with sphinxes to the Lower Terrace, a zone of transition between the profane and the sacred. This was a garden with myrrh trees and fountains, as though a foretaste of that which endures in the desert of the other world. A pair of lions (the left-hand one survives) stood at the bottom of the ramp leading up to the Middle Terrace and another pair (the right-hand one survives) stood at the top. These were at once guardians of the temple and witnesses to the rising sun, proof of rebirth."

Colonnades and pillars to the north and south of the lower ramp, at the western end of the lower platform were decorated with reliefs of the queen. The Queen is shown with Tuthmose III, her Co-Regent at the time of its building, whose name was included in the original decorations. Reliefs on the Northern Colonnade depict garden themes and water birds caught in nets. The South Colonnade tells the story of her two obelisks that were cut at Aswan and set up at Karnak. At both ends of the colonnades, Osiride statues of the Queen were placed.

The first ramp led to the Middle Platform and Second Court. At its center, a second ramp rose to the upper platform. The northwestern enclosure wall held a single colonnade, the "True Norther Colonnade" with 15 columns and behind 4 square massive pillars facing the cliff to the north. Equally too, there were 4 undecorated chambers behind this line of columns. At the western end of this Second Court housing the Middle Colonnade beyond the square pillars, reliefs depict her "Divine Birth" to the north and "Punt Expedition" to the south. At the northern and southern extremes of these depictions are the Anubis and Hathor shrines, right and left respectively. The Chapel of Anubis has a hall with 12 "Proto-Doric" columns with simple capitals. Here the chiseled-out features of Hatshepsut are shown with Anubis and the Sun God with his wife

HATSHEPSUT'S TEMPLE AT DEIR EL BAHARI

Hathor. At the opposite end of the colonnade, the Hathor Chapel has two halls with 8 pillars and 8 columns in the outer hall. There are 4 columns at the Hathor Portico and 12 columns in the inner hall. Two additional columns are in the sanctuary area. These areas suffered both from the destructive forces of Tuthmose III's vengeance and from the time of the Akhnaton Revolution. Here, Haag (1987: 242) notes, Hatshepsut "meets Amun, she suckles generating milk from Hathor, and above a recess in the left wall she and Tuthmosis III are shown kneeling, she to the left with an offering of milk, he to the right with wine. Also, within this chamber, in a little alcove on the right and towards the floor, is a figure of Senmut, Hatshepsut's favorite."

Deir el Bahari 32. What an interesting site of syncretistic art symbolism.

FREDERICK MONDERSON

Deir el Bahari 33. Visitors admire pillar and column in the Hathor Shrine. Some columns are smooth though decorated and others are Proto-Doric with sixteen sides.

Between the two chapels, the "Birth Colonnade" to the north and the "Punt Colonnade" to the south are two rows of square pillars. Haag (1987: 240) has again written: "On the walls of the Birth Colonnade (north) are reliefs depicting Hatshepsut's divine parentage: Amun has assumed the form of her father who sits facing Ahmosis, her mother, on a couch. The couple gazes at one another, their knees touching in a scene at once conventional and reserved and yet sensitively conveying their ardor. The Queen is led to the birth chamber, accompanied by strange deities, a smile of suffering

HATSHEPSUT'S TEMPLE AT DEIR EL BAHARI

and delight playing on her lips. The child, conventionally shown as a boy, is fashioned by Khnum on his potter's wheel, and also its Ka. Just as Tuthmosis III justified his claim to the throne with the story of Amun's selection of him at the Temple of Karnak, so these reliefs serve the same purpose for Hatshepsut." Naturally, Hatshepsut's story preceded those of both Thutmose III at Karnak and Amenhotep III at Luxor. These were all 18th Dynasty monarchs.

The "Punt Colonnade" depicts the expedition to Punt on the coast of Somaliland. Some books now say this land is in Ethiopia. Further, Haag (1987: 241) tells us of the bounty of the voyage, as the ships return to Thebes, "very heavily with marvels of the country of Punt; all goodly fragrant woods of god's land, heaps of myrrh resin, of green myrrh trees, with ebony and pure ivory, with green gold of Emu, with cinnamon wood, with incense, eye cosmetic, with baboons, monkeys, dogs, with skins of the southern panther, with natives and their children. Never was the like of this brought for any pharaoh who has been since the beginning."

The "Second Ramp" led to the "Upper Platform." A Polish Expeditionary team has long been restoring this area. Previously closed to the public, it is now finished and open to visitors. Two colonnades of 22 each alternating 16-sided "Proto-Doric" columns behind and square pillars with Osiride figures of the Queen are met at the ramp's entranceway on the Upper Terrace. Most of these Osiride Figures have been destroyed. Nearly half a dozen have been restored and the bases of many are evident. A granite doorway gives access to the colonnaded Upper Court.

Maspero (1926: 100) has written of the area of the main court: "… on the left, is the covered court where sacrifices were offered to the deceased queen, and on the right is another court, in which stands the altar, one of the very few found in situ in Egypt. It is rectangular, made of fine limestone and measures 16 feet by 13 feet. A flight of ten steps on the western side leads to the top, which is 5 feet above the pavement, and surmounted by a heavy cornice."

FREDERICK MONDERSON

Deir el Bahari 34. Proto-Doric and round columns in the Hathor Shrine.

Deir el Bahari 34a. Erik Monderson beside the *in situ* altar with its ten steps dedicated to Ra-Horakhty.

HATSHEPSUT'S TEMPLE AT DEIR EL BAHARI

In "The Main Hypostyle Hall of the Temple of Hatshepsut at Deir el Bahari" Leszek Dabrowski (*Journal of Egyptian Archaeology* 56, 1970: 101) states, regarding work of clearance at the Upper Court, "At the time when the work was being started there lay on the court of the Third Terrace many fragments of columns which supposedly had come from the former hypostyle hall. Probably they had been brought over with some purpose. The columns were distinguished by an unusual form, hitherto unknown. They were sixteen-sided, proto-Doric, but with a broad band of relief on one side through almost the whole length. The band was topped by a representation of the Horus-falcon. Similar columns have as yet not been found elsewhere in Egypt; they are markedly different from all the others."

This is again confirmed by Z. Sysocki who concluded in "The Upper Court Colonnade of Hatshepsut's Temple at Deir el Bahari" *Journal of Egyptian Archaeology* Vol. 66 (1980: 69) stating: "There are original fragments of the unique type of polygonal columns which appeared in Egypt only in the Upper Court of the mortuary temple of Queen Hatshepsut." That is, after he had summed up his findings regarding the Upper Court Colonnade in the following:

1. All the columns of the court had the same diameter at the base, about 80 cm, and the same height, about 495 cm.

2. Only columns surrounding the open court were decorated with panels covered with figurative and hieroglyphic relief. On the other hand, the remaining columns were standard polygonal columns with sixteen sides having the same proportions but without panels.

3. The court colonnade probably had two rows of columns on the south, east and north side and three rows on the west side.

4. The columns with smaller dimensions, which are preserved in a few fragments, could not have belonged to the court

colonnade and if they belonged to it, they must have been put in characteristic places and on a socle.

The Upper Platform Court is surrounded by a now roofless hypostyle colonnade consisting of 108 columns that enclose the Court from four sides. There are 2 rows of 14 to the front and 4 to the rear or east and west. Then there are 3 rows of 4 each, north and south or right and left. Thus, the Court is encircled by 108 columns. Off to the left is the Sanctuary of Hatshepsut. In the opposite direction on the right is the Sanctuary of the Sun God Ra-Horakhty. To the western end of the upper platform and abutting the face of the cliff is a row of 18 niches with Osiride statues of the queen. Hewn into the overhead cliff, in the northwest and southwest are two chapels of Amun.

The beauty of the temple and success of the architect lies in his alternation of architectural features making this structure unique. So much so, in approaching the functional temple, ancients saw couchant lions, sandstone sphinxes, gardens, and pools, Osiride Statues of the Pharaoh, and numerous pillars and columns. Aldred (1987: 164) mentions: "Over 200 statues in various stones of different sizes were furnished for the temple precincts."

Even today, 3500 years later the aura of its majesty still mystifies. The temple supplies a view of mystique and wonderment evident to both ancient and modern visitors. Smith sums it up best when he writes (1959) Deir el-Bahari, "combines a broad feeling of openness of space with a nicety of architectural detail. This only gradually becomes apparent as one approach into the individual parts."

The beautiful lady, Hatshepsut, Ma'at-Ka-Ra, is today a source of inspiration to all women. This is especially so for the woman of African descent. What Hatshepsut represented is a constant reminder to modern African women of what can be accomplished with mind, daring, beauty and charm. These traits seem to enhance delegation of authority, administrative abilities and respect and adoration of the Gods as well as the people.

HATSHEPSUT'S TEMPLE AT DEIR EL BAHARI

Deir el Bahari 35. Balloon over the columns of the Hathor Shrine.

Deir el Bahari 36. Columns of the Hathor Shrine showing restoration.

FREDERICK MONDERSON

Deir el Bahari 37. Looking out at the two kinds of columns and the square pillars of the Hathor Shrine.

REFERENCES

Aldred, Cyril. *The Egyptians*. New York: Thames and Hudson, (1961) 1987.

_____. *Egyptian Art*. New York: Oxford University Press, 1980.

Bratton, Fred G. *A History of Egyptian Archaeology*. New York: Thomas Y. Crowell Company, 1968.

Breasted, James H. *The History of Egypt*. New York: Scribner's, (1905) 1909.

_____. *Ancient Records of Egypt*. 5 Vols. *The Eighteenth Dynasty* II. New York: Russell and Russell, Inc., (1906) 1962.

Brier, Bob. *Ancient Egyptian Magic*. New York: Quill, (1972) 1981.

Clarke, Sommers and R. Engelbach. *Ancient Egyptian Construction and Architecture*. New York: Dover Publications, Inc., (1930) 1990.

Gardiner, Alan. *Egypt of the Pharaohs*. New York: Oxford University Press, (1961) 1974.

Haag, Michael. *Guide to Egypt*. London: Michael Haag, Ltd., 1987.

HATSHEPSUT'S TEMPLE AT DEIR EL BAHARI

Hobson, Christine. *The World of the Pharaohs*. New York: Thames and Hudson, 1987.
Kamil, Jill. *Luxor: A Guide to Ancient Thebes*. 2nd Edition. London: Longman, (1973) 1980.
Kees, Hermann. *Ancient Egypt: A Cultural Topography*. Chicago: University of Chicago Press, (1961) 1977.
Lesko, R. Switalski. "The Senmut Problem." *Journal American Research Center in Egypt* VI (1967: 113-18.)
Lurker, Manfred. *The Gods and Symbols of Ancient Egypt*. New York: Thames and Hudson, (1974) 1991.
Maspero, Gaston. *Manual of Egyptian Archaeology*. New York: G. P. Putnam's Sons, 1926.
Mertz, Barbara. *Black Land, Red Land*. New York: Dodd and Mead, (1966) 1978.
Mokhtar, Wafaa Moh. *Karnak*. 2nd Edition. Cairo: ND.
Murnane, W. J. *The Penguin Guide to Ancient Egypt*. New York: Penguin Books, 1983.
Murray, M. A. *The Splendor That Was Egypt*. New York: Philosophical Library, (1949) 1957.
Rogers, J.A. *The World's Great Men of Color*. Vol. I. New York: Macmillan, (1957) 1972.
Smith, W. Stevenson. *The Art and Architecture of Ancient Egypt*. New York: Penguin Books, (1958) 1981.
Steindorff, George and Keith C. Seele. *When Egypt Ruled the East*. Chicago: University of Chicago Press, (1942) 1971.
Trigger, B. G. and B. J. Kemp, D. O'Connor, A. B. Lloyd. *Ancient Egypt: A Social History*. New York: Cambridge University Press, (1983) 1989.
Wilson, J. A. *The Culture of Ancient Egypt*. Chicago: University of Chicago Press, (1951) 1959.
Woldering, Irmgard. *The Art of Egypt: In Time of the Pharaohs*. New York: Greystone Press, 1963.

FREDERICK MONDERSON

Deir el Bahari 38. Defaced figures, probably Gods who could have been defaced during the Amarna Revolution; and defaced figure of the Queen found in the Upper Court.

In any classic love story, there is equally the case of the male, sometimes as equally wonderful. This must be told for it completes the picture of how people lived in other times and what the African ancestors did and how they felt. The good side of their experiences can always have something that can teach and edify us. Of course, the bad side also can let us learn how to avoid such similar debacles. Nevertheless, we must continue to make the connection and establish the link with ancient Africa and teach our people, young and old, for this is a powerful legacy that the ancestors have left us. Remember ancient Africans were the originators of science, technology, medicine, art and architecture, astronomy, quarrying and working in stone, religious belief and practice, and a whole lot of other fields of knowledge. This is why the Afrocentrists argue, particularly Dr. Diop, the history of Africa will be meaningless unless it is incorporated with that of ancient Egypt/Kemet. This is essential to the proper effort of African historiographic reconstruction. Dr. Diop also said African scholars who refuse to link Egypt to Africa are either neurotics or educated fools. Our work is cut out for us because the European world is vigorously defending Egypt as their cultural legacy. This is so, these moderns argue, because their capitals are inundated with museums and other collections of ancient African artifacts generally acquired dubiously

HATSHEPSUT'S TEMPLE AT DEIR EL BAHARI

in the age of imperialism that was not simply political, social, and economic but also intellectual. Now!

Nevertheless, whoever suggested that behind every successful man is a woman probably never suspected behind the earliest successful woman there were several men, particularly a man named Senmut? This support is particularly important today, as the African woman struggles upward and yet cannot get that true African man to stand with and respect them, for whatever reason. This partnership is important. It is the potent complementarity of the African male/female principle at work. In Theban theology, the Sun and Earth as husband and wife and the Moon as son formed a successful triad. The harmony generated in this family relationship has and still has far-reaching implications for religious, philosophic and spiritual syncretism. Without one, there is no other!

Deir el Bahari 40 and 41. The Queen, in Blue or War Crown, makes a Presentation of contrite heart, probably, to deities of the Temple (left); and, another defaced figure of the Queen (left). Even the Maat Ka Ra cartouches have been violated.

FREDERICK MONDERSON

7. Senmut - Architect of Queen Hatshepsut
By
Frederick Monderson

Senmut was an Egyptian nobleman who lived during the reign of Queen Hatshepsut in the XVIII Dynasty, about 1490-1470 B.C. He came from a poor family as told by Petrie (1923: 47) argued, but luck, intelligence, fortune and hard work helped him reach the top in the early Nile Valley culture experience. The ancient records indicate his family history was 'not in writing.' His lowly background or humble beginnings is surmised from the in-elaborate tomb he built for his family. Some scholars think Senmut was a scribe. Others, as Aldred (1962: 252) believe he was a general in the army of the Queen's father Thutmose I, and this background was helpful to both parties. He notes: "Hatshepsut loved her father who made her co-regent with Thutmose II. Still, the old king was aware that she would have political and social difficulties in the male dominated world of the pharaohs. Possibly, Thutmose I may have advised her alliance with 'strong males' in the kingdom. Therefore, her close alignment with Senmut and other principal male figures during the era of her dominance in the nation's political life was arguably, shrewd policy."

This part of the essay attempts to sketch some aspects of the life and seeks to identify the works of a great African who helped an assertive Queen hold the reins of power in a male dominated world. He remained her strongest ally and supporter during the exciting years of female daring and architectural and artistic creativity with a measure of political astuteness. With Senmut's help she galvanized a nation, created lasting architectural constructions, mystified commentators over the centuries and motivated modern women wanting to be like the "First Queen." In addition, some of the more significant references are included in this piece to

HATSHEPSUT'S TEMPLE AT DEIR EL BAHARI

encourage further research particularly by young writers and scholars.

At a very young age, the queen married Thutmose II, as was customary. At that time, Winlock (1928: 47) wrote, "to look upon her was more beautiful than anything; her splendor and her form were divine; she was a maiden, beautiful and blooming." Winlock (1928: 48) says further, she was styled: "The Great Princess favored with charm, Mistress of all Lands, Royal Daughter and Sister, Great Royal Wife, Lady of the Two Lands, Hatshepsut."

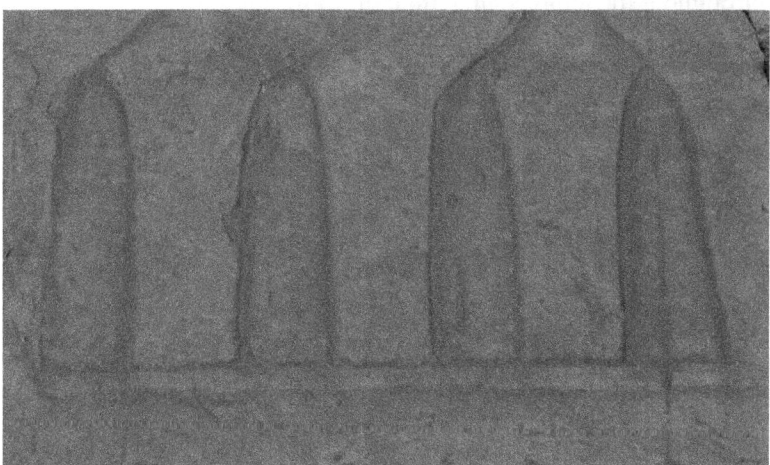

Deir el Bahari 41a. The four Obelisks Hatshepsut erected at Karnak, across the river. Remember, the orientation of this temple and Karnak temple seems in alignment.

Deir el Bahari 42. One of the many images of Senmut scattered throughout the temple, an unthought-of idea.

Deir el Bahari 42a. Nile Gods uniting the Land under Queen Hatshepsut.

HATSHEPSUT'S TEMPLE AT DEIR EL BAHARI

Deir el Bahari 42b. Lap-wings beneath the Nile Gods as they unite the land under the ruler.

Deir el Bahari 43. Beside the Hathor Shrine, boats and individuals create an air of excitement, anxiety and gaiety.

FREDERICK MONDERSON

Deir el Bahari 44. Still another figure of the Queen that has suffered some form of damage.

Her marriage to Thutmose II produced a girl child named Nefru-re. When Thutmose II died, she pushed aside young Thutmose III, her stepbrother and co-regent, the natural heir. She made herself ruler of all Egypt. Shortly after she claimed to be the Son of the God Amun and declared herself "King of Upper and Lower Egypt." Many people believed Senmut was behind all this since; he headed a political party aligned with powerful individuals in the country.

Whatever his origins, Senmut or Senenmut whose name means "mother's brother," and the factors of his rise to prominence in ancient Kemet, he was well liked by Hatshepsut, Ma'at-Ka-Ra. Many believed he was her lover! Throughout their close association, the Queen bestowed on him some 40 titles, and he

HATSHEPSUT'S TEMPLE AT DEIR EL BAHARI

became the most powerful man in the kingdom during her reign. Hayes (1959: 106) attributes to him such titles as Minister of Finance, Minister of Works, Hereditary Prince and Count, Wearer of the Royal Seal, and Sole Companion. Breasted (1962: 350-51) listed other titles as Great Father, Tutor of the Princess Nefru-re, Conductor of Festivals, Overseer of the Garden of Amun, Chief Steward of the King, Overseer of the Prophet of Montu, Overseer of Administrative Offices and Imy-Weret Priest. Winlock (1928: 50) says this Steward of Amon, became Overseer of Amon's Granaries, Storehouses, Fields, Cattle, and Slaves as well as Controller of the Hall of Amon, and Overseer of all the Works of the King in the Temple of Amon as well. Again, Winlock (1928: 50-52) wrote: "Once he was firmly established in Hatshepsut's favor, we find him controlling the wealth of the royal family in the same detailed way. Starting as High Steward of the two queens, Hatshepsut and her little daughter Neferure, he became in time Controller, Overseer of All of the Works of the King; Superintendent of the Royal Slaves, of the Treasury, of the Armory, and of the Red Crown Castle. Hence it came about not only did he boast of being Governor of the Royal Palace, but he tells us that he was Superintendent of the Private Apartments, of the Bathroom, and of the Royal Bedrooms as well. These few, yet significant, titles indicate the tremendous power and influence he came to wield during this period of female remodeling and assertiveness in the XVIIIth Dynasty."

Senmut's fame as an architect puts him among other great builders during the New Empire. Architects of significance were also associated with the pharaohs Amenhotep III and Thutmose III of the Eighteenth Dynasty and the Ramesside builders Rameses I, Seti I, and Rameses II, of the Nineteenth Dynasty as well as Rameses III of the Twentieth Dynasty.

Though Senmut built a tomb early in his adult life, at a later time he built another one. The first was dug out of the hillside above the village of Sheikh Abd-el-Qurna. This elaborate tomb (No. 71), built before he became a powerful individual in the kingdom, writes

FREDERICK MONDERSON

Kanawati (1981: 27) was "decorated with scenes of the Egyptian afterlife." Equally, Breasted (1909: 272) pointed out: "Senmut employed several bright colors such as yellow, blue, red and green in its decoration." His family members and household helpers as well as his horse and a pet ape, were buried in and around the tomb. Mertz (1978: 46) indicates his pet horse, a mare, was twelve-and-a-half-hands high.

Deir el Bahari 45. Measuring the Gum of Punt before being given as gifts to the Egyptians.

A *Scientific American* (1937) article entitled: "Egypt's Oldest Horse Found Buried in Huge Thebes Tomb" states: "The horse was, in the time of Senmut, a recent importation from Asia into Egypt, and it is natural that anyone who owned a horse would have prized an animal so spirited as compared with the lowly donkey, which up to that time had been the only animal of the sort in Egypt."

Archaeologists who found the horse wrapped in linen also discovered a saddle thought to be the oldest in the world. The pet ape was identified as a cynocephalus by Ambrose Lansing and William C. Hayes, leaders of the Metropolitan Museum of Art's expedition to Thebes. They explained, the "animal had been carefully wrapped and buried just as though it were a child, and in the coffin had been placed a saucer of raisins. Its owner; whether Senmut or another had evidently been very fond of his pet monkey. Evidence seems to indicate both animals were mummified."

HATSHEPSUT'S TEMPLE AT DEIR EL BAHARI

From the site of Senmut's first tomb, No. 71, we know the names of his father Ramose, 'The Worthy,' and his mother, Hatnufer, 'Lady of the House.' His beloved sister was Ahotep 'The Justified.' Amenhotep, a younger brother and Harmose, a musician, with his lute lying beside his coffin, were all buried here. Also interred here were a young servant and an old woman Prophetess of the God Amun. He had another sister whose name is missing.

Senmut had another brother, Senmen, Davies argued, who was probably older. He too seems to have had royal children as protégé. His charge was Senenyah and probably also Nefru-re. Senmen was also buried on a very steep slope of the hill at Sheikh Abu-el-Qurna, where Senmut was probably later interred. There was a third brother, Pairy.

Davies (1913: 282) seems to identify Senmen with what became a unique phenomenon, particularly in American history. His description of this sight at Abu-el-Qurna is quite interesting, for he states: "Higher upon, on the same hill-side, is a feature unique in the necropolis, a group of man, woman and child, carved out of a great boulder, the back of which is still left in the rough." Three thousand years later, American Presidents would be glorified in this Mount Rushmore phenomenon, an African replica.

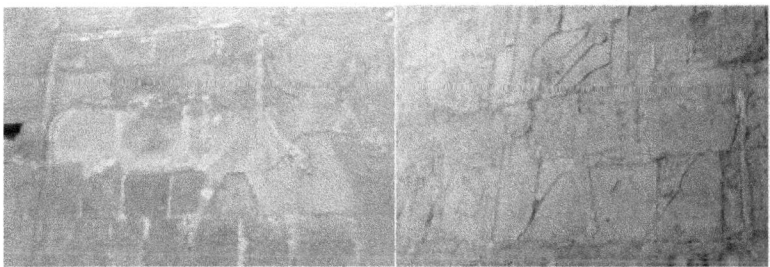

Deir el Bahari 46. A Hathor Cow on the southern wall of Hathor Shrine. Great praises have been heaped on these figures for their originality and realism (left); and, another "Cow of Deir el Bahari" being fed by the hand of a defaced individual.

FREDERICK MONDERSON

Senmut had several close friends, Breasted (1962, II: 350-51) indicated, who helped the Queen consolidate her power and rule the country. Their names were Nehsi, Chancellor, who led the famous expedition to Punt. Thutiy and Thutnofre were Treasurers. Puyemre was the Second Prophet of Amun. Hapu-Seneb was the Vizier or Prime Minister. Ineby was the Viceroy of Nubia. Dewaemhen was the First Herald, and Tenenre, a scribe.

While Senmut's many talents amassed tremendous political, social, and religious power, his greatest fame seems to come from his administrative and architectural accomplishments. Breasted (1909: 274) assigns to him the construction of the Queen's architectural masterpiece, her Funerary or Mortuary Temple at Deir-el-Bahari. "Located on the West Bank of the Nile at Thebes, it lies near the XIth Dynasty Temple of Mentuhotep II, for which it served as model, five hundred years later. Here Senmut had his second tomb, with a long sloping corridor, secretly dug under the Queen's temple."

Deir el Bahari 47. The Upper Court, 360 Degrees.

HATSHEPSUT'S TEMPLE AT DEIR EL BAHARI

Deir el Bahari 47a. The Upper Court, 360 Degrees.

Deir el Bahari 47b. The Upper Court, 360 Degrees.

FREDERICK MONDERSON

Deir el Bahari 47c. The Upper Court, 360 Degrees.

Deir el Bahari 47d. The Upper Court, 360 Degrees.

HATSHEPSUT'S TEMPLE AT DEIR EL BAHARI

Deir el Bahari 47e. The Upper Court, 360 Degrees.

Deir el Bahari 47f. The Upper Court, 360 Degrees.

FREDERICK MONDERSON

Deir el Bahari 47g. The Upper Court, 360 Degrees.

Deir el Bahari 47h. The Upper Court, 360 Degrees.

HATSHEPSUT'S TEMPLE AT DEIR EL BAHARI

Deir el Bahari 47i. The Upper Court, 360 Degrees.

Deir el Bahari 47j. The Upper Court, 360 Degrees.

FREDERICK MONDERSON

Deir el Bahari 47k. The Upper Court, 360 Degrees.

Deir el Bahari 47l. The Upper Court, 360 Degrees.

HATSHEPSUT'S TEMPLE AT DEIR EL BAHARI

Deir el Bahari 48. Another and better view of the "Cow of Deir el Bahari" with Pharaonic motifs of Dominion, Life and Stability.

This tomb, styled Theban Tomb 353 by today's count, was located to the Northeast of the First Ramp in the First Court. This was indeed a bold move. Dorman (1988) describes the tomb as being "entirely rock cut and conforms to a simple, if unorthodox, ground plan: Three chambers laid out sequentially in an essentially linear configuration to which access is gained."

FREDERICK MONDERSON

Deir el Bahari 48a. The Upper Court, 360 Degrees.

Deir el Bahari 48b. Representation of Thutmose I and his mother Senseneb.

HATSHEPSUT'S TEMPLE AT DEIR EL BAHARI

Deir el Bahari 49. Broken Cartouche with names partly destroyed.

Deir el Bahari 50. Right half of the Lower Colonnade. While it's agreed the Lower Colonnade comprised square pillars on the outside and round columns on the inside. Unfortunately, all of the round columns on this half of the Lower Colonnade have been broken.

Such a daring act by a commoner seeking to juxtapose himself within the Mortuary Temple of the Pharaoh was unthinkable. Kees (1977: 255-56), elaborating on such an unthinkable act for a commoner, commented how, equally Senmut "dared to have figures of himself carved behind the doors of the chapel-shrines, such as the rock-shrine of Hathor, and to have a new rock-tomb cut for himself under the forecourt of the temple so that he could rest within the sacred precinct." Hayes (1959: 107) who excavated his tomb pointed out how, Senmut also: "inscribed his name some 70 times in out of the way places in the Queen's mortuary temple."

Deir el Bahari 51. Shrine of Anubis. Columns with lintel or base, Proto-Doric pattern and without capital.

The secret tomb was unfinished and abandoned following his downfall in the nineteenth year of her rule. Only one chamber with four walls had been decorated. Here he placed inscriptions of the *Book of the Underworld, Book of the Gates* and *Book of the Dead*. The potency of his religious beliefs is underscored by Winlock (1928: 37) who wrote, the contents of these books "guided the soul in the life to come when it voyaged with the sun across the ocean of

HATSHEPSUT'S TEMPLE AT DEIR EL BAHARI

the night, penetrated the fearsome corridors of Hades, or cultivated the Elysian Fields."

Another outstanding feature of Tomb 353 was its ceiling with one of the earliest astronomical charts ever found. This was, naturally, before the beautiful chart found in Seti I's tomb. Its significance and relevance for astronomy is underscored by Winlock (1928: 37) who wrote: "In the center of the northern half appears the bull-headed constellation 'Meskhetiu'- our "Great Bear" and the circumpolar star groups. Across the sky the twelve ancient monthly festivals are drawn, each as a circle with its round of twenty-four hours and below, the celestial bodies of the northern sky pass in procession. Opposite, in the southern skies Orion stubbornly turns his face away from the smiling Sothis, who chases after him, beckoning fruitlessly year after year. Above them, in turn, come the lists of the decans with the name of Hatshepsut herself introduced among the heavenly beings."

Therefore, from his reposed Osirian rest this great Black man would gaze heavenward and behold his beloved Black woman in the celestial realm. What a profound praise of African womanhood! We are told this secret tomb was later discovered, defaced and destroyed by Thutmose III's forces.

More important, however, it's as if Senmut anticipated such a fate at the hands of his adversaries for the role he played in the Queen's seizure of power and rule on the great throne. The walls of his tomb were decorated and then had plaster placed over them. Then he inscribed a second set of decorations. The defacement of Thutmose III's forces mutilated the top layer of decorations. The plaster protected the bottom layer and with the passage of time, as it began to peel, scholars who found the tomb came to recognize the wisdom of the man and his strategy.

The Queen's Funerary Temple at Deir el-Bahari, of which Dr. Yosef ben-Jochannan (1989) wonders why it never became a wonder of the ancient world, is an enduring work of art because of the

FREDERICK MONDERSON

innovative feat of Senmut's construction. The structure had lower and middle colonnades and three platforms rising into the background hills. Another colonnade was located in the upper reaches of the northern enclosure wall. There were also two ramps and the Sanctuary was located on the upper platform. Here the "Holy of Holies" resided. Throughout the magnificent structure, Senmut placed many columns, sandstone sphinxes and Osiride statues of the Queen. In an early age when most buildings were single stories, this three-story structure was quite an innovation.

At a later time, during the Greco-Roman period we see many temples built on the spot of older temples because these places were already sacred from earlier times. Since Deir el-Bahari held the 11th Dynasty temple of Mentuhotep II who was deified in the 12th Dynasty, this may have been the principal reason for the choice of this spot. Equally too, the architectural prototype was already laid out, and Senmut's genius like that of Imhotep at the Step-Pyramid, was to add innovations to the Deir el Bahari prototype. Nevertheless, and significant, in the former architect's case, his innovations had no prototype. Another reason for use of this location may have been the manifestation of the Sun God Ra on the valley with the hills as a backdrop. This divine intervention is also shown in the goddess Hathor who is often depicted as coming out of the hills of Deir el-Bahari.

Petrie (1884: 6-7) gives a most unique description of the play of the sun on this remarkable structure and location. He wrote the splendor of the Egyptian sunsets displays a variety of tints unaccustomed in most countries. "As the sun nears the horizon, the eastern cliffs of the valley appear rich in yellow light with purple shadows deepening to crimson at sunset; there rises a bright rosy band across the eastern sky, higher and higher as the light wanes, with the dark blue of night below it, and the brightness of the day still above. This fades as it nears the zenith, and then the western sky from a golden glow darkens to a rich tawny brown, fading into purple, and so to blue, on either side; this brown, however, never gives place to blue, but gradually becoming spangled with the stars it deepens to blackness of night."

HATSHEPSUT'S TEMPLE AT DEIR EL BAHARI

Deir el Bahari 52 and 53. Shrine of Anubis. The God of the Dead enthroned before a sumptuous "Table of Offerings;" and Raised relief figure of the God of the Dead.

W. Stephenson Smith's (1959: 233) view is, the temple "combines a broad feeling of openness of space with a nicety of architectural detail which only gradually becomes apparent as one penetrates into the individual parts."

On the north side of the temple the Anubis Shrine stands near the Northern Colonnade. A little south of this area and closer to the center of the temple is located the colonnade of the Queen's "Divine Birth," near or right of the Second Ramp. Equally just across, on the south side of the upper reaches of the Middle Colonnade to the left of the same Ramp is the Punt Colonnade where the famous expedition is recorded.

The genius of Senmut is reflected in his combining of square pillars and polygonal columns. Smith (1959: 233) again confesses, the "variation between pillar and column is one of the reasons for

FREDERICK MONDERSON

Senmut's success in employing the polygonal channeled column, which had long been one of the happiest of Egyptian inventions."

The architect's fame is not confined to this masterpiece. Senmut cut two obelisks from the Aswan quarries in the south. This was quite a feat. Aswan always had good stone. It supplied red, black and grey granite stone to practically every serious building effort nationwide. In the fifteenth or sixteenth year of her rule, the Queen tells us, according to Breasted (1962, II: 317) states: "I sat in the palace, I remembered him who fashioned me, my heart led me to make for him two obelisks of electrum whose points mingled with heaven." Electrum was an alloy of gold and silver. It has also been called white gold, for the more silver added, the whiter it gets.

Senmut left his name at Aswan, the place of good stone where many pharaohs quarried hard stone for their more important monuments. Benson and Gourlay (1898: 165) commented on Senmut's name at this location. They wrote, "his stele at Aswan shows him standing before Hatshepsut, and entitled the Royal Seal Bearer, the Companion, Greatly Beloved, Keeper of the Palace, Keeper of the Heart of the Queen, Making Content the Lady of Both Lands, Making All Things Come to Pass for Her Majesty. It is stated that he there carved the two great obelisks for the Queen."

Deir el Bahari 54. View of the buses now at a distance and the "Tap Tap," one pound each per ride, to ferry visitors to the temple.

HATSHEPSUT'S TEMPLE AT DEIR EL BAHARI

Deir el Bahari 55. Shrine of Anubis. Amun enthroned, before a sumptuous Table of Offerings.

In commentary on this extraordinary feat, Margaret Murray (1957: 50) is of the view: "To quarry two obelisks of a hundred feet in length by the arduous method of pounding, to transport them to the river and load them on a fleet of boats, to erect them in their places, engrave and polish them, and all in the space of seven months, was a triumph of organization." Senmut had them erected across the river on the east bank at Karnak, Thebes. One still stands to this day. The apex of another lies about one hundred feet away in front of the "Coca Cola Temple" just in front of the Sacred Lake. Another obelisk was abandoned at Aswan because, after several months of work, a fault was discovered in its base. Today, it is styled the "unfinished obelisk" and credited to the Queen, because her Cartouche (Shennu) is there. Cartouche or Shennu is an oval containing her name. As an aside, the Queen's cartouche was also discovered in the courtyard pavement of Edfu Temple, on bricks re-used in the building of that temple. Because of the significance of the find of a piece of the queen's temple, with her name on it, in a temple more than a thousand years later, the piece was removed to the Cairo Museum, where it now resides.

Deir el Bahari 56. Shrine of Anubis. Sanctuary of the Shrine of the God of the Dead, with surprisingly good color. In the rear, two figures stand before Amun.

HATSHEPSUT'S TEMPLE AT DEIR EL BAHARI

Senmut also organized the expedition of ships to the land of Punt, in Central East Africa, today's Somaliland. Depicted on the temple walls at Deir el-Bahari, this successful voyage brought back spices, ebony, ivory, apes, and panther-skins, cattle and incense trees. Incense trees, depicted in the inscriptions on the walls of the temple were planted on the upper terrace of the temple. Today there is still evidence of two incense trees planted at the entrance pylon to the First Court.

Senmut's greatness is not only measured in his wonderful works of architecture, quarrying, expedition and love for the Queen and her daughter; but also, in his role as "power behind the throne" at a very challenging and exciting time of revolution and female daring creative progress in the ancient African world.

Many statues of Senmut have survived and are considered exceptional works of art. Some show him seated, squatting or standing with his royal charge, Nofru-re. In addition, Aldred (1980: 158) is an authority on Egyptian art and has written: "Five sculptures of various sizes show him kneeling to offer a huge sistrum to the goddess Hathor or Mut, evidently the first of a type of statue that gained in popularity thereafter."

Dorman (1988) mentions some 25 existing statues of Senmut carved in materials of a wide variety including diorite, red quartzite, gray-black quartzite, yellow sandstone, gray granite, pink granite, yellow quartzite, alabaster, gray-green schist, red porphyry, and bedrock and bedrock-limestone shale. Further, the modern universalism of this ancient African genius is reflected in the widespread location of his statues. One each is located in the British, Brooklyn, Cairo and Chicago Museums. There are the Deir Rumi and Edfu Statues, as well as others at Fort Worth, Gebel Silsila, Geneva and the *Karakol Magazine* at Karnak. The Louvre, Metropolitan Museum of Art of New York and Munich Museum are included, and another is named after the archaeologist Naville. The *Sheikh Labib* Magazine has one and another is in his tomb No. 71.

FREDERICK MONDERSON

Deir el Bahari 57. Tuthmose III, *Men Khepper Ra* makes a Presentation of two jars to Sokar, a God of the Dead.

What else did he do; is a question one may ask. Well, he built the following architectural monuments as identified by Dorman (1988) that includes some of those already mentioned. Tomb 71, at Sheikh Abd el-Qurna; (2) Tomb 353, at Deir-el-Bahari; (3) Stela from Tomb 71, Berlin 2066; (4) Donation Stela from North Karnak; (5) Sinai Stela of Neferura from Serabit el Khadem, Cairo JDE 38546; (6) Cenotaph at Gebel el Silsila; (7) Graffito at Sehel Island, Aswan; (8) Graffito in Metropolitan Museum of Art, Tomb 504 at Western Thebes; (9) Temple at Deir el Bahari; (10) Gateway in Precinct of Temple of Mut at Karnak; (11) Tomb of Tjay.

In addition, a number of miscellaneous objects of his, and containing his name, according to Dorman are as follows, (1) Sarcophagus MMA 31.3.95; (2) Alabaster Unguent Vase, British Museum 29333; (3) Whip Handle, MMA 23.3.46; (4) Decorated Staff, Berlin 14348; (5) Limestone Rubber in MacGregor

HATSHEPSUT'S TEMPLE AT DEIR EL BAHARI

Collection; (6) Granite Rubber in MacGregor Collection; (7) Sandstone Rubber, Berlin 15086; (8) Quartzite Sandstone Rubber, British Museum EA 33890; (9) Two Glass Beads, British Museum EA 262.89-90; (10) White Amethyst Bead MMA 26.7.746; (11) Carnelian Hathor Amulet, Brooklyn 61.1.92; (12) Cylinder Seal in University College London; (13) Cylinder Seal in Boston Museum of Fine Arts, 67.1137; (14) Alabaster Model Saucer from Tomb 353, MMA 27.3.488; (15) Alabaster Model Saucer from Tomb 353, Cairo JDE 51830; (16) Tomb Sealings Davies and Macadam Corpus No. 84, 88, 261; (17) Hieratic Tablet; (18) Ostraca; (19) Name Stones of Senmut; (20) Name Stones of Hatshepsut with Hieratic Docket. This is indeed an impressive tally for one person.

Soon after many of these events Thutmose III deposed Queen Hatshepsut, around the nineteenth year of her reign. Thutmose, in anger, wrecked her temple, tomb and statues. In many places the young king, according to Breasted (1909: 283) "erased her inscriptions." The tomb she built in the Valley of the Kings, where she hoped to be buried, was destroyed. The tunnel from Deir el-Bahari, she is thought to have begun so she could be taken directly from the Mortuary Temple to her tomb, is still discussed today for its engineering, philosophical, theological and cosmological daring. Much of this is credited to our hero.

Deir el Bahari 58. Cartouche of Thutmose III, Men-Khepper-Ra, with a portion of the Suten Bat symbol just to the left.

FREDERICK MONDERSON

Senmut and those who tied their fate to that of the Queen received the same treatment of desecration. Breasted (1962 II: 348) has shown: "On Senmut's Berlin statue, on his Karnak statue, in his tomb, on his tombstone, and in the Punt reliefs, his name is chiseled out. In the Punt relief, his entire figure, and those of his two companions, Nehsi and Thutiy, likewise ardent supporters of the Queen are chiseled out."

Deir el Bahari 59. Close-up of northern half of the Lower Colonnade with pillars to in front and destroyed columns in the rear.

The architect's second tomb, under the temple, was discovered, defaced and destroyed. As a result, he was probably buried in the first tomb at Sheikh Abu el-Qurna with his relatives. Nevertheless, his intelligence and daring allows us to remember how hard work helped a poor child make it great in the North-Eastern African country, ancient Kemet.

Appropriately, a concluding epithet in praise of man's glorification and praise of a beautiful African woman is aptly included, as he said: "'I was one upon whose utterances his Lord relied, with whose advice the Mistress of the Two Lands was satisfied, and the heart of the Divine Consort was completely filled. I was a noble to whom one harkened, for I repeated the words of the King to the companions. I was one whose steps were known in the palace, a

HATSHEPSUT'S TEMPLE AT DEIR EL BAHARI

real confidant of the Ruler, entering in love and coming forth in favor, making glad the heart of the Sovereign every day. I was the one useful to the King, faithful to the God, and without blemish before the people. I was one to whom was given the Inundation that I might control the Nile; one to whom the affairs of the Two Lands were confided. That which the South and the North contributed was under my seal and the labor of all countries was under my charge. And moreover, I had access to all the writings of the prophets - there was nothing from the beginning of time which I did not know.'"

Modern commentators have speculated on the probable causes of the actions of Senmut. Some people blame Senmut for "vainglory" in flaunting his titles as an exaggeration of power and influence. Others either blame Tuthmose III and his party or even Queen Hatshepsut for the final destruction and defacement much of his works and name have experienced. One thing is perfectly clear; the nobleman supported the Lady beyond reasonable limits. Quite probably she could not make it in the male dominated world with its potential for treachery had it not been for Senmut. Maybe another architect and his achievements would not have been as permanent and magnificent. Possibly Senmut's love for the lady was the quintessential ingredient that dictated and motivated his many efforts.

Deir el Bahari 60. A better view of the columns of the Shrine of Anubis and, some believe, the "unfinished" Northern Colonnade with its 15 columns.

FREDERICK MONDERSON

Deir el Bahari 61. Another view of the previous photo showing the "True Northern Colonnade" with its 15 columns and unfinished architrave and three small rooms at their rear thought to be places for worship of deities of the temple. The seams give indication of original size and shape of the blocks before being pounded into desired arrangement.

REFERENCE

Aldred, Cyril. *The Egyptians*. New York: Thames and Hudson, (1962) 1980.
ben-Jochannan, Yosef. *Abu Simbel to Ghizeh*. Baltimore: Black Classics Press, 1989.
Benson, Margaret and Janet Gourlay. *The Temple of Mut in Asher*. London: John Murray, 1898.
Breasted, James H. *A History of Egypt*. New York: Scribner's, (1905) 1909.
_____. *Ancient Records of Egypt*. 5 Vols. *The Eighteenth Dynasty* II. New York: Russell and Russell, Inc., (1906) 1962.
Davies, N. Deg. "The Tomb of Senmen, Brother of Senmut." *Society of Biblical Archaeology* 35 (December 10, 1913: 282-85).
Dorman, Peter F. *The Monuments of Senmut*. London: Kegan Paul, International, 1988.

HATSHEPSUT'S TEMPLE AT DEIR EL BAHARI

"Egypt's Oldest Horse Found Buried in Huge Thebes Tomb." *Scientific American* (January 30, 1937: 68-69).
Hayes, William C. *The Scepter of Egypt* Vol. II. New York: Metropolitan Museum of Art, 1959.
Kanawati, Labib. *The Tomb and its Significance in Ancient Egypt.* Cairo: Prism, 1987.
Kees, Herman. *Egypt: A Cultural Topography.* Chicago: University of Chicago Press, 1977.
Mertz, Barbara. *Red Land, Black Land.* New York: Dodd, Mead, (1966) 1978.
Murray, Margaret. *The Splendor That Was Egypt.* New York: Philosophical Library, (1949) 1957.
Petrie, W.M. Flinders. *The Arts of Ancient Egypt: A Lecture.* London: Field and Tuer, 1884.
_____. *Social Life in Ancient Egypt.* New York: Houghton Mifflin Company, 1923.
Smith, W. Stephenson. *The Art and Architecture of Ancient Egypt.* New York: Penguin Books, (1958) 1989.
Winlock, H.E. "The Egyptian Expedition 1925-1927: The Museum's Excavations at Thebes." *Metropolitan Museum of Art Bulletin* 23 (1928: 3-58).

Deir el Bahari 62. Gods who came to witness the phenomenal "divine birth" of Hatshepsut as depicted on the walls of the "Birth Colonnade."

FREDERICK MONDERSON

Deir el Bahari 63. Events on the northern Middle or Birth Colonnade. Divinity pours libation over the now defaced figure of Hatshepsut with Tuthmose III looking on. In the right frame, Ra Horakhty looks at the erased figure of the Queen.

Deir el Bahari 63a. Shawki Abdel Rady, Egyptian Guide to the Antiquities also called "The Black," who knows more than most about the truly indigenous history of the Ancient Egyptians.

HATSHEPSUT'S TEMPLE AT DEIR EL BAHARI

8. "IMPORTANT ARCHAEOLOGICAL DISCOVERIES IN EGYPT." London *Times* Thursday, August 4, 1881. Cairo. July 24, 1881.

Besides being memorable for the appearance of the comets, the year 1881 must ever hold a high place in the annals of Egyptological discovery. Monsieur Maspero, the recently appointed director of the Boulak Museum, is at the present moment in Paris actively engaged in preparing for publication the texts of the pyramids of the Fifth and Sixth dynasties, which were opened last spring at Sakkara.

The forthcoming number of his "Recueil" will contain the entire text of the pyramid of King Ounas, the last king of the Fifth dynasty. But the saying that "it never rains but it pours" may be now fairly applied to archaeological discovery. Long before the savants have had time to peruse, ponder over, or profit by the wonders unearthed at Sakkara they are now suddenly overwhelmed with a fresh supply of material in the form of the largest papyri yet known, and by the apparition of the mummies, with all their mortuary appendages and inscriptions, of no less than 30 Royal personages. This discovery which had just been made calls for special interest in England, for among the 30 Royal mummies are to be found those of King Thutmose III and of King Rameses II-it was the former who ordered the construction of the obelisk which now stands upon the Thames Embankment, and it was the latter who, 270 years afterwards, caused his own official titles and honors to be inscribed upon its faces besides those of Thotmes III. These two monarchs now lie side by side in the Boulak Museum, and even the flowers and garlands which were placed in their coffins may to-day be seen encircling the masks which cover the faces of the deceased just as they were left by the mourners over 3,000 years ago.

FREDERICK MONDERSON

Deir el Bahari 64. A better close-up look at divinity pouring libation over the erased figure of the Queen while Tuthmose III, who stood behind her, looks unscathed.

Deir el Bahari 65. A more panoramic view of the starry ceiling, uraei with disks, the libation scene and head of Amun on a column.

Last June Daoud Pasha, Governor of the province of Keneh, which includes the ancient Theban district, noticed that the Bedaween offered for sale an unusual quantity of antiquities at absurdly low prices. The Pasha soon discovered that the source of their hidden treasure was situated in a gorge of the mountain range, which separates Deir-el-Bahari from the Bab-el-Malook. This gorge is situated about four miles from the Nile to the east of Thebes. Daoud Pasha at once telegraphed to the Khedive, who forthwith dispatched to the spot Herr Emil Brugsch, a younger brother of Dr. Henry Brugsch Pasha, who, during Monsieur Maspero's absence in Paris,

HATSHEPSUT'S TEMPLE AT DEIR EL BAHARI

is in charge of all archaeological excavations in Egypt. Herr Brugsch discovered in the cliffs of the Libyan mountains, near the Temple of Deir-el-Bahari, or the "Northern Convent," a pit, about 35 ft. deep, cut in the solid rock; a secret opening from this pit led to a gallery nearly 200 ft. long, also hewn out of the solid rock. This gallery was filled with relics of the Theban dynasties. Every indication leads to the conviction that these sacred relics had been removed from their appropriate places in the various tombs and temples, and concealed in this secret subterranean gallery by the Egyptian priests to preserve them from being destroyed by some foreign invader. In all probability Cambyses, thus they concealed them at the time of the invasion of Egypt. Herr Brugsch at once telegraphed for a steamer, which on Friday last safely deposited her precious cargo at the Boulak Museum.

Deir el Bahari 66. As the Goddess Hathor stands nearby, midwife goddesses lead the pregnant mother of Hatshepsut (center) to the birth chamber.

FREDERICK MONDERSON

Deir el Bahari 67. Sullied Queen Hatshepsut reaches to salute Goddess Hathor.

HATSHEPSUT'S TEMPLE AT DEIR EL BAHARI

Deir el Bahari 67a. While a goddess tends the Queen who holds the new-born, the Mid-wife goddesses hold the twin Ka's of the divine birth child Hatshepsut.

Deir el Bahari 67b. Some of the Goddesses holding some of the 12 Kas of Hatshepsut.

Deir el Bahari 67c. More of the Goddesses holding more of the "12 Kas" of Hatshepsut.

FREDERICK MONDERSON

Deir el Bahari 67d. Even more Goddesses holding some of Hatshepsut's Kas.

Deir el Bahari 67e. More of the same scene in the Birth Colonnade.

Deir el Bahari 67f. Divinities handing over the two Kas of the baby Hatshepsut to more divinities and to the right, Thoth hands the young Queen over to Amun. Much defacement is visible.

HATSHEPSUT'S TEMPLE AT DEIR EL BAHARI

Deir el Bahari 67g. Presentation of the Queen's double Ka to the enthroned gods.

FREDERICK MONDERSON

Deir el Bahari 67h. A defaced Hatshepsut stands before Osiris with his symbols while to the right, Goddess Hathor stands in colorful garb all below a starry ski and with uraei with disks.

The full value of this discovery, of course, cannot as yet be determined. The papyri have not yet been unrolled, nor have the mummies been unwrapped. The following Theban Sovereigns are the most important of those mummies Herr Brugsch has identified:
-

HATSHEPSUT'S TEMPLE AT DEIR EL BAHARI

Aahmes I (Amosis), 1st King of the 18th Dynasty, reigned B.C. 1700 (about).
Amenhotep I (Amenophis), 2nd King of 18th Dynasty, reigned B.C. 1666 (about).
Thotmes I, 3rd King of 18th Dynasty, reigned B.C. 1633 (about).
Thotmes II, 4th King of 18th Dynasty, reigned B.C. 1600 (about).
Thotmes III (the Great), 5th King of 18th Dynasty, reigned B.C. 1600 (about).
Ra---meses I, 1st King of 19th Dynasty, reigned B.C. 1400 (about).
Seti I, 2nd King of 19th Dynasty, reigned B.C. 1366 (about).
Rameses II (the Great), 3rd King of 19th Dynasty, reigned B.C. 1333 (about).
Pinotem, 3rd King of 21st Dynasty, reigned B.C. 1033 (about).
Raskhenen (Dynasty and date of reign unknown).
Queen Ra-Ma-Ka (Hatasou?).
Queen Aahmes Nofert Ari.

Conspicuous by its massive gold ornamentation, in which cartouches are set in precious stones, is the coffin containing the mummy of Maut Nedjem, a daughter of King Rameses II. An alabaster canopic urn, containing the heart and entrails of the deceased, accompanies each of the mummies.

Deir el Bahari 68 and 69. Starry ceiling, uraei with disks with uraei and disks with wings, defaced cartouches and top of a "Proto-Doric" column (left); figure of Hatshepsut with face disfigured as she stands before defaced Hathor, near her Shrine (right).

FREDERICK MONDERSON

Four papyri were found in the gallery at Deir-el-Bahari, each in a perfect state of preservation. The largest of these papyri-that found in the coffin of Queen Ra-ma-ka is most beautifully illustrated with colored illuminations. It is about 16 in. wide, and when unrolled will probably measure from 100 to 140 feet in length. The other papyri are somewhat narrower, but are more closely written upon. These papyri will probably prove to be the most valuable portion of the discovery, for in the present state of Egyptology a papyrus may be of more importance than an entire temple, and, as the late Maurice Pasha used to say, "it is certain that if ever one of these discoveries that bring about a revolution in science should be made in Egyptology, the world will be indebted for it to a papyrus."

No less than 3,700 mortuary statues have been found which bear royal cartouches and inscriptions. Nearly 2,000 other objects have been discovered. One of the most remarkable relics is an enormous leather tent, which bears the cartouche of King Pinotem, of the 21st dynasty. This tent is in a truly wonderful state of preservation. The workmanship is beautiful. It is covered with hieroglyphs most carefully embroidered in red, green, and yellow leather. The colors are quite fresh and bright. In each of the corners is represented the royal vulture and stars.

Deir el Bahari 70. The two temples of Hatshepsut and Mentuhotep.

HATSHEPSUT'S TEMPLE AT DEIR EL BAHARI

Deir el Bahari 70a. Hatshepsut in Red Crown (left), and again being embraced by the God Amon.

Fifteen enormous wigs for ceremonial occasions form a striking feature of the Deir-el-Bahari collection. These wigs are nearly 2 ft. high, and are composed of frizzled and curled hair. There are many marked points of resemblance between the legal institutions of ancient Egypt and of England. For instance, pleadings must be

FREDERICK MONDERSON

"Traversed," "confessed and avoided" or demurred to. Marriage settlements and the doctrines of uses and trusts prevailed in ancient Egypt, but the wearing of these wigs was not extended to the members of the legal profession, but was reserved exclusively for the princess of the blood and ladies of very high rank.

Deir el Bahari 70b. To the left Amon embraces the Queen and right, he embraces Hatshepsut in Double Crown.

It is curious to recall the fact that when Belzoni, in 1817, discovered at Bab-el-Malook the tomb of Seti I - a tomb which has since been popularly called "Belzoni's tomb"- a fine sarcophagus in alabaster stood in the furthest chamber. This sarcophagus was subsequently brought to England, and is now in Sir Joan Soane's Museum. Herr Brugsch has now brought to light the original occupant of this sarcophagus, who may now be seen at the Boulak Museum, near his son, Rameses II.

HATSHEPSUT'S TEMPLE AT DEIR EL BAHARI

Herr Brugsch assures me that he believes that there is another secret gallery leading from the pit at Deir-el-Bahari. When M. Maspero returns next October, further excavations will doubtless be undertaken, but the Boulak Museum, so suddenly enriched as it has been during the present year, now occupies a position not inferior to any in Europe.

Deir el Bahari 70c. A native guide stands near a pillar of Hatshepsut being embraced by Amon (left) and Amon holding scepter and ankh (right).

FREDERICK MONDERSON

Deir el Bahari 70d. Amon and Amon on a Pillar with a decorated back wall as part of the "Birth Colonnade."

Deir el Bahari 70e. Starry ceiling, uraei with disks, Table of Offerings, flying hawk with talons grasping a ring, all in surprisingly good color.

HATSHEPSUT'S TEMPLE AT DEIR EL BAHARI

Deir el Bahari 70f. Amon and Amon on pillars in the Temple of Hatshepsut.

FREDERICK MONDERSON

Deir el Bahari 70g. Wearing the Osiris Crown, White Crown, Horns, feathers and disk, Hatshepsut holds a scepter and mace in the left hand and gestures with the right while striking a pose customarily done in reviewing her troops. Notice her tail behind.

HATSHEPSUT'S TEMPLE AT DEIR EL BAHARI

Deir el Bahari 70h. Faces, foreign and Egyptian, sign for foreign country, stability and ankh.

Deir el Bahari 70i. Another of the images of the Queen that escaped the wrath of her enemies, where she wears a beard, necklace and holds symbols of her power.

HATSHEPSUT'S TEMPLE AT DEIR EL BAHARI

Deir el Bahari 70j. View of tourists examining the columns and art in the Hathor Shrine.

Deir el Bahari 70k. The hawk in a serekh and heads of foreigners.

FREDERICK MONDERSON

Deir el Bahari 70l. Cartouches of Thutmose III, *Men-Kheper-Ra* and *Thutmose*, still preserved with good color.

Deir el Bahari 70m. Hathor head column with cow's ears and wig-hairpiece surmounted above with miniature building housing uraei with horns and disks while in the backdrop the mountain rests below the blue sky.

HATSHEPSUT'S TEMPLE AT DEIR EL BAHARI

Deir el Bahari 71. Looking out from the Hathor Shrine, square pillars and round columns.

Deir el Bahari 71a. Umbrella of a visitor admiring pillars and Hathor-headed columns in the Hathor Shrine with the mountain as a back-drop.

FREDERICK MONDERSON

Deir el Bahari 71b. Hathor-headed column close-up with two cow face uraei sporting horns and disks surmounting the abacus.

In a note by the author of this work, the mummy of the personage, Maat-Ka-Ra is not the famous Queen Hatshepsut, builder of the Deir el Bahari temple, but a later princess. It was customary to choose names of previous and illustrious ancestors as in this case. The body of the Ma'at Ka Ra, Hatshepsut, has not been found and it's believed that the zealots of Thutmose III destroyed the Queen's person as they defaced her images and much of her works.

HATSHEPSUT'S TEMPLE AT DEIR EL BAHARI

Deir el Bahari 71c. Looking past the columns to the Sanctuary (behind the white cloth over the grated opening) beneath the mountain backdrop.

FREDERICK MONDERSON

Deir el Bahari 72. Ful view of the reconstructed temple as visitors enter the entrance gallery.

HATSHEPSUT'S TEMPLE AT DEIR EL BAHARI

9. "The Discovery at Thebes, Egypt." *The Academy* 20 No. 484 (August 13, 1881:127).

A great sepulchral treasure, upon which the daily Papers have of late been reporting with more or less accuracy, has been brought to light at Thebes. Some misconception having prevailed with regard to the identity of the royal mummies, and the way in which the discovery was brought about, readers of the ACADEMY, will doubtless be glad to know the exact particulars.

Deir el Bahari 73. Tuthmose III, Men-Khepper-Ra, wearing the Red Crown, embraced by two divinities and to the right, Hatshepsut enthroned.

Observing how, for the last ten years, relics of great value and rarity have been steadily finding their way from Egypt to Europe, Prof. Maspero had long suspected the Arabs of having found a royal tomb. When, however, an English traveler presented him, some

FREDERICK MONDERSON

little time ago, with a photographed reproduction of the first pages of a superb Ritual bought at Thebes, and that Ritual proved to be the funeral papyrus of Pinotem I, his suspicion became certainty, and he determined to get at the bottom of the mystery. Having succeeded Mariette-Pasha as Director and Conservator to his Highness the Khedive, Prof. Maspero proceeded last spring to make his first official trip to Upper Egypt. Arrived at Thebes, and confident that he had laid his finger upon the right man, he at once ordered the arrest of a certain well known dealer and guide called Abd-er-Rasoul. This man (who, with his two younger brothers, lives in the tombs behind the Ramesseum) was then conveyed to the district prison at Keneh, where for two months he maintained an obstinate silence. The other brothers, meanwhile, had the trade to themselves, and fraternal jealousy at last moved the captive to betray their joint secret. Hereupon the Governor of Keneh telegraphed to Cairo. By this time Prof. Maspero had left for Europe; but Herr Emil Brugsch, Keeper of the Museum at Boolak, and Ahmed-Effendi-Kemal, the acting secretary and interpreter, started immediately for Thebes, and transported the treasure to Cairo. I am indebted for these details to Prof. Maspero, from whom I have received a long and interesting letter dated August 4. Believing that he will not object, I translate word for word his account of the objects discovered. "We have put our hands not upon a royal tomb, but upon a hiding place in which were piled - perhaps after the great tomb robberies of the Twentieth Dynasty, or more probably at the time when Thebes was sacked by the Assyrians-thirty-six mummies of kings, queens, princes, and high-priests. Thus, we have the mummy of a Raskenen; that of Amenophis I and of his wife Ahmes-Nefertari; that of Thothmes II; of Rameses XII; of Pinotem I; of the Queen Isi-m-Kheb; of the Queen Notemit, &c., &c.; the whole representing some 6,000 new objects, including five papyri, one of which is the funeral papyrus of the Queen Makere, of the Twentieth Dynasty, and two plaques similar to those I have already published, and which, by-the-way, must have come from this source."

HATSHEPSUT'S TEMPLE AT DEIR EL BAHARI

Deir el Bahari 74. The apex of Queen Hatshepsut's standing Obelisk at Karnak Temple, across the river.

FREDERICK MONDERSON

Rameses XII, it may be observed, was the 'Pharaoh who dispatched the Ark of Khonsu to Mesopotamia for the cure of the Princess Bakatana' - see De Rouge, Sur une Stele Egyptienne (1858), and Birch on "The Possessed Princess," *Records of the Past*, vol. iv (1875); and Pinotem I was grandson and successor of Herihor, the usurping high-priest and chief prophet of Amen who deposed the successors of Rameses XII. Pinotem reigned, according to Brugsch, for twenty-five years, and was conquered by the Assyrians under that leader whom the author of the *Geschichte Aegyptens* styles "the great king of kings." Pinotem, possibly as a matter of policy, called his grandson by the throne-name of Thothmes III, and his granddaughter by the throne name of Queen Hatasu. Hence the very natural error of the *Times* correspondent at Cairo, who believed he beheld in the newly discovered Ra-men-Kheper and Remaka, the great Pharaoh and Queen of the Eighteenth Dynasty. The history of this same Ra-men-Kheper is also curious. While Pinotem, his grandfather, was at Tanis, awaiting the Assyrians, he was dispatched to Upper Egypt to put down an insurrection at Thebes; but at Thebes his first act was to recall the banished Ramessides, and to accept his ancestor's former rank of high-priest of Amen. After this, we meet with some more princes of the names of Rameses, ending with a Rameses XVI. Princess Ramaka, whose name is written Karamat by Brugsch, married Shishak I, and so became Queen of Egypt.

And now we ask, what has become of the mummies of all the missing Pharaohs between Raskenen and Pinotem I? Where are the other Amenhoteps, the other Thothmes, and the other Ramessides? Have they been dispersed or are they still hidden in some cavern not yet discovered? Mariette-Pasha, it will be remembered long ago advanced a theory, that the great temples on the west bank opposite Luxor and Karnak were to be regarded as memorial - chapels pertaining to the tombs of their founders in Bab-el-Molook; and he even suggested that subterraneous galleries might possibly connect these temples with their tombs at the other side of the mountain. The hiding-place just found is said to be behind the Temple of Hatasu, at Deir-el-Baharee. It may yet prove to lead through the heart of the mountain into some tomb in the valley of the tombs of

HATSHEPSUT'S TEMPLE AT DEIR EL BAHARI

the kings; and may not similar tunnels exist in connection with the Temples of Goorneh and Medinet-Haboo and the Ramesseum?

Deir el Bahari 75. Hatshepsut in Karnak. The Queen's standing obelisk (right) beside that of her father, Thutmose I (left) in the illustrious Hall of Columns that would experience much redecorating under Thutmose III.

There can, I imagine, be little doubt that the Prince of Wales's beautiful papyrus (which is still on view in the long Egyptian gallery at the British Museum) came from the hiding-place, which has just yielded its treasure to Boolak. Amelia B. Edwards.

FREDERICK MONDERSON

Deir el Bahari 76. Hatshepsut in Karnak. A closer look at the Queen's standing obelisk in all its glory.

10. "The Archaeological Discovery at Thebes, Egypt." *The Academy* 20 (August 27, 1881: 167-68).

In reply to numerous letters of enquiry from various quarters, I hasten to place before readers of the *Academy* some additional particulars of the great discovery at Thebes, promising that I am indebted for this intelligence to the great courtesy of Prof. Maspero, who permits me to publish the facts under the authority of his name.

It seems, unfortunately, but too certain that the discovery - though of immense importance per se - is in some respects less startling than it appeared to be on the first report; and that those correspondents who have confidently proclaimed the finding of the greatest Pharaohs of the Eighteenth and Nineteenth Dynasties will

HATSHEPSUT'S TEMPLE AT DEIR EL BAHARI

have to admit that they were too readily misled by appearances. The mummy-cases when first discovered were piled in the utmost disorder in a small chamber measuring some twenty-three feet by thirteen. They had evidently been opened and searched by the Arabs, and have doubtless been despoiled of many precious things. Several mummy-cases are found not to belong to their present occupants, the names on the cases not corresponding to the names on the bandages of the mummies. Thus, a certain Princess Merit-Amen lies in the coffin of a priest named Sonoo; Queen Ansera (Eighteenth Dynasty) lies in the coffin of the Lady Rai, who was nurse to Queen Ahmes-Nofrotari; and Pinotem II lies in a coffin which bears the cartouche of Thothmes I. Other mummy-cases are empty-as, for instance, that of Rameses I; while the coffin of a Princess Mashontimoohoo contains a false mummy, in the shape of a piece of wood enveloped in bandages to represent an actual corpse. The Arabs are doubtless answerable for much of this displacement and confusion; and most of the mummies, their bandages and amulets, will need careful scrutiny before their identity can be positively determined.

Deir el Bahari 77. Figure in White Crown, embraced by two divinities and the defaced cartouche indicates its Hatshepsut. To the right, the enthroned figure is Hatshepsut before the Table of Offerings.

FREDERICK MONDERSON

As regards the two to which public attention has been chiefly directed - namely, the mummies supposed to be those of Thothmes III and Rameses II - they are precisely those which present the most difficulties, and are consequently the most doubtful. The mummy-case, which bears the cartouche of Ra-men-Kheper, has evidently been broken open at some remote date. It was found to contain objects bearing the cartouches of Thothmes III, and there would therefore seem to be grounds for believing that it really is the mummy-case of that great Pharaoh. But then the occupant of this case is of most ambiguous aspect, and measures only 1 meter 55 centimeters in length. Supposing even that the process of mummification may have had the effect of somewhat reducing the corpse, it is difficult to believe that this mighty hero could have shrunk to a stature of something like 61 inches. The mummy-case attributed to Rameses II is described by Prof. Maspero as being of unpainted wood, bearing a royal effigy, of which the eyes, the uraeus serpent, the beard, scepter, and whip, are colored black. On the breast are two cartouches which read Rameses Mer Amen, Ra-user-Ma-Sotep-en-Ra, but which are not spelled with precisely the same hieroglyphic characters as the names of Rameses the Great. "It is this personage," writes Prof. Maspero, "whom it has been sought to identify with Rameses II. To this identification I see many objections, the chief of which is based on the fact that the mummy-case, which is of very fine workmanship, presents every characteristic of mummy cases of the Twentieth Dynasty, including the orthography of the cartouches, in which we find the special form of N (represented by the crown symbolical of Lower Egypt) which was in use at that epoch. The face of the effigy, which was usually sculptured in the likeness of the deceased, does not present the aquiline and well-known type of Rameses II. I am therefore disposed to believe, in the absence of fresh evidence that we behold in this king not Rameses the Great but his namesake Rameses XII of the Twentieth Dynasty, who was the Pharaoh of the stela of Bakhtan. Here, however, as in the case of the mummy discovered in the coffin of Thothmes III, it will be necessary minutely to investigate every detail of the bandages and minor objects before arriving at a definite decision as to the identity of the personage."

HATSHEPSUT'S TEMPLE AT DEIR EL BAHARI

Deir el Bahari 78. Visitors take photographs in the Second Court before the Second Ramp leading to the Upper Terrace and its Upper Colonnade with standing colossal Osiride Figures. The opening leads to the Upper Court.

Prof. Maspero describes the hiding-place as situated behind an angle of the cliff a little way to the southwest of Deir-el-Bahari, and so well concealed that one might have passed it twenty times without ever suspecting its existence. The mouth of the pit is about 60 meters above the level of the plain, and the shaft descends perpendicularly to a depth of 12 meters. Hence a gallery 74 meters by 4. Seeing that the hieratic inscriptions on the mummy-cases of Seti I and Rameses XII state that these bodies were, for safety, deposited in the tomb of Queen Ansera; seeing, also, that the mummy of this Queen has been found here, though reposing, as before mentioned, in the coffin of the Lady Rai; Prof. Maspero suggests that the excavation may very possibly have been the original tomb of that Sovereign.

Finally, the number of mummies actually recovered is not thirty-six, but twenty-nine. Of these seven are kings, nine are queens and princesses, and five are personages of distinction. Those mummies belonging to the Eighteenth and Nineteenth Dynasties would seem to have been removed hither from their graves in the Valley of the

FREDERICK MONDERSON

Tombs of the Kings during the reign of Her-Hor, the first priest-king; and the place was evidently thenceforth used (perhaps because the times were troubled) as the burial-vault of his descendants and successors. Amelia B. Edwards.

Deir el Bahari 79. Polish Egyptian Archaeological and Conservation Mission of the Deir el Bahari Temple that did mostly restoration of the Upper Terrace, Upper Court and Sanctuary area.

11. "A Waif from Dayr-el-Baharee."
The Academy 22 (August 26, 1882: 157).

Kindly grant me space to report an interesting little discovery which I have had the good fortune to make, and which casts another sidelight upon the famous find at Dayr-al-Baharee. In four "canopic" jars belonging to G. Briscoe Eyre, Esq., I have identified the sepulchral vases of Pinotem I, second priest-king of the Her-Hor Dynasty. Mr. Eyre purchased these vases at Luxor in 1874. They are of fine alabaster, and stand about fifteen inches high. Each vase is engraved with a short legend in three vertical columns, the hieroglyphs being filled in with blue. The inscriptions read as follows: -

1. The Osiris, High Priest of Amen, Beloved of the Great God Amset, Pinotem, justified before Ptah.

HATSHEPSUT'S TEMPLE AT DEIR EL BAHARI

2. The Osiris, High Priest of-Amen, Beloved of the Great God Hapi, Pinotem, justified before the Gods.
3. The Osiris, High Priest of Amen, Beloved of the Great God Taumautef, Pinotem, justified before Osiris.
4. The Osiris, High Priest of Amen, Beloved of the Great God Qebhsenuf, Pinotem, justified before Ptah.

The name not being enclosed in a royal oval, it is evident that we here have the vases of Pinotem I, who ranked as Pontiff only. He was son to the High Priest Piankhi, and grandson to Her-Hor; and he stands third in order of succession. His mummy, it will be remembered, was found at Dayr-al-Baharee, enclosed in two wooden sarcophagi; and it was during the sixth, tenth, and sixteenth years of his reign, and by his command, that the mummies of Amenhotep I, Thothmes II, Rameses I, Seti I, and Rameses II were inspected, removed from place to place, and had their "funerary appointments" renewed, by a commission of dignitaries and scribes, who recorded these facts and dates upon the coffins and bandages of the illustrious dead. Nor must we forget that it was in consequence of Col. Campbell's purchase of the funeral papyrus of this same Pontiff that Prof. Maspero was last year enabled to trace the plunderers of the Her-Hor vault (see the *Academy*, No. 484, August 13, 1881).

Three of Mr. Eyre's vases are empty; but the fourth (Amset) is yet unopened, and doubtless contains part of the viscera of Pinotem I. Amelia B. Edwards.

FREDERICK MONDERSON

Deir el Bahari 80. The Author in the Second Court and some of the many visitors to the Temple. Notice the Second Ramp completely repaired as opposed to its state in Photo Deir el Bahari 17, Page 84,

12. "The Excavations at Dayr el Bahari." EGYPT EXPLORATION FUND. *The Academy* 44 No. 1104 (July 1, 1893: 17-18).

For the first time since the Egypt Exploration Fund has existed, the society had received permission to excavate one of the temples of Thebes. It is an urgent duty for me to express my gratitude to M. de Morgan, the present director of the Ghizeh Museum, not only for having granted to the society one of the choicest spots in Egypt, but also for having considerably facilitated my work by lending me a tramway. It is absolutely necessary to have one in such a place, where the debris have to be carried to a considerable distance, in order to be quite sure that nothing of interest is being hidden in the course of the work.

All travelers who have been at Thebes know the majestic cliff, in the form of an amphitheater, at the foot of which is Dayr el Bahari

HATSHEPSUT'S TEMPLE AT DEIR EL BAHARI

(the Northern Convent), known by that name since the Copts built a convent over the ruins of the old sanctuary. The temple is quite different from all others in Egypt, being built in successive terraces, the highest of which leans against the mountain on its northern and western sides. The length of the temple was much greater than its width; the sanctuary was a rock-cut chamber, in the axis of the building, and opened on the upper terrace.

Deir el Bahari 81. Lower, Middle and Upper Colonnades in view.

Mariette first excavated the temple. Following the central avenue which leads to the sanctuary, he cleared a great part of the southern side, throwing over on to the northern side all the rubbish which he could not get rid of. The most important part of his discoveries consisted of the supporting wall of the upper terrace, with sculptures depicting a naval expedition to the land of Punt; the rock-cut sanctuary of the goddess Hathor, where the goddess is seen in the form of a cow, suckling the young queen, Hatshepsu, or Hatasu as she is incorrectly called; and the great hall of offerings. On the northern side, Mariette, and after him M. Maspero, dug out part of the portico at the foot of the upper terrace, and a small sanctuary corresponding to that of Hathor, which was found full of mummies of recent date.

FREDERICK MONDERSON

I settled near Dayr el Bahari at the end of January, and started work at once in the part, which Mariette had left, untouched and covered with mounds of rubbish. I began with the upper terrain. I was obliged, owing to the steep slope, to establish two lines of tramway, the upper one carrying the rubbish to a short distance, the lower one taking it a long way off, to what is called the *Birket,* a large depression used in former times as a clay pit. Though I could not work so long as I wished, having been stopped by the fast of Ramadan, the excavations led to important results. I cleared completely the northern half of the upper terrace, the description of which was quite unknown, and which is separated from the rest by a stout wall preserved only in its lower part. This wall, in which there are two doors, is the southern limit of a part of the building, having a decidedly funerary character. I suppose it was connected with the burial-place of Thothmes I, which is perhaps somewhere in the neighborhood.

The western door leads to a long hall with well-preserved sculptures of gigantic proportions, showing Hatasu and Thothmes III making offerings to Amon. Next to it is an open court limited on the north by the mountain, on the east by the remains of a chamber with columns. From that court one enters into a small rock-out chapel, the funeral chapel of Thothmes I. The ceiling, well painted in blue with yellow stars, is an Egyptian arch. The revolutionary king, and after him the Copts, have scratched out the figures of the gods Osiris, Anubis, etc.; but the king is well preserved. He is seen there with two different queens: one of them, Ahmes, is well known; the other one, Senseneb, so far as I know, has not yet been met with. An iron door has been put to the chapel by the authorities of the Ghizeh Museum.

Just before the door of this chapel is a building unique of its kind among Egyptian temples. It is a great square altar in limestone, to which access is given by a flight of steps. Until I discovered the staircase, I was in doubt as to the nature of the building. I thought at first that it might be a mastaba, the construction which covers the tombs in the Old Empire. The people who plundered the temple in ancient times evidently had the same idea, for they pulled down a

HATSHEPSUT'S TEMPLE AT DEIR EL BAHARI

corner of it, in order to see whether it concealed a pit. All my doubts were removed when I could read the inscription. It says that a royal person who is clearly Queen Hatasu, though her name is hammered out – "built a large altar in white stone to her father, Ra Harmakhis;" meaning perhaps her deified father, Thothmes I. The altar is a platform, 16 feet by 13 feet and 5 feet high, with ten steps leading up to it. It had a low parapet like the terraces, in order to prevent the offerings from falling into the court, and probably there was a smaller altar in hard stone placed on the top. It is the only altar of this kind known in Egypt. Mr. John Newberry, who, as an expert in architecture, gave me most valuable assistance, put back again some of the stones that had been thrown down by the plunderers; and, as all the blocks seem to be there, we hope to be able to restore the altar nearly complete next winter.

Deir el Bahari 82. Visitor takes a breather near colossal Osiride Figures of the Queen as a security guard, with rifle, sits to the rear.

FREDERICK MONDERSON

Deir el Bahari 83. One of the reconstructed portrait head of Queen Hatshepsut that has survived her enemies' and other miscreants' assaults on the woman and temple.

Another object, also unique, I found on a terrace above the chambers excavated by M. Maspero. It is one of the sides of a large shrine of ebony, more than six feet high, erected by Thothmes II. Ebony never being found in large pieces, the whole panel is made of small fragments held together by ebony pegs, which have been used with the greatest skill as part of the sculpture. This shrine was erected by Thothmes II, who says in the Inscription that it was made of ebony "from the top of the mountains" in honor of his father, Amon. But everywhere the figure of Amon has been cut out with a knife, evidently by the revolutionary king. It is the same with another part of the shrine which I discovered close by, a leaf of the folding door which closed it, which has rings of bronze for the bolt. It was a very difficult and delicate task to lift out the panel and to pack it, without running the risk of seeing the whole thing fall to pieces, as ebony is a very heavy wood. However, we succeeded in removing it without

HATSHEPSUT'S TEMPLE AT DEIR EL BAHARI

the slightest injury from the terrace where it had been lying for many centuries. It was encircled in a double frame and carefully packed in a box, made under Mr. Newberry's supervision. It is now on its way to the Ghizeh Museum, where it will have to be repaired by a skilled cabinet-maker before being exhibited.

Deir el Bahari 84. Another view of the above portrait head showing the Queen wearing the White Crown.

The Copts who built their convent over the temple have practiced the most ruthless destruction among the very beautiful sculptures, which adorned it. They have scattered all over the building parts of a most interesting scene, which I believe belonged to the lowest terrace. Some of its fragments are built into walls; others have been used as thresholds or stairs, others piled together with capitals and bricks in the clumsy partitions, which they raised between the rooms of the convent. I carefully gathered and stored all the blocks I found belonging to that series which represented the transportation of obelisks and other heavy monuments. The most interesting of these

FREDERICK MONDERSON

Deir el Bahari 85. Close-up of one of the Osiride Figures of the Queen.

blocks show an obelisk lying on a high boat, where it has been placed by means of a sort of sledge on which it still rests. A small

HATSHEPSUT'S TEMPLE AT DEIR EL BAHARI

one rowed by several men tows the high boat. Unfortunately, the block is small; we [see] only the top of the obelisk, but we may hope next winter to find the remaining parts. It is the first time anything has been discovered relating to the transportation of obelisks.

The last thing I found is a very curious inscription concerning the birth of Hatasu and her ascension to the throne. It is on the supporting wall of the upper terrace. We see the god Anubis rolling an enormous egg, and goddesses suckling the young queen; further we come to her enthronement by her father. Thothmes I is seen in a shrine, stretching forth his hands towards a young man, who is the queen. The young man is hammered out, but still discernible, as well as the long inscription which accompanies the pictures and which relates how Thothmes called together the grandees of his kingdom, and ordered them to obey his daughter. There is an obscure allusion to his death and a description of the rejoicings when she ascended the throne. The date, I believe, may be interpreted in this way: that the first of the month Thoth, the first day of the variable year, and the beginning of the seasons, or of the natural year, fell on the same day.

This short summary shows how rich a place is Dayr el Bahari, and how much we may expect from further excavations, which I hope will be resumed in the autumn. I must add that in the rubbish I found a great many Coptic letters written on potsherds or on pieces of limestone. They contain the correspondence between certain monks called Victor, John, Abraham, Zacharia, etc. They usually begin with a salutation, and sometimes with the formula: "In the name of the Father, of the Son, and of the Holy Ghost." These letters have all been sent to Europe, and are the property of the Fund.
EDOUARD NAVILLE.

FREDERICK MONDERSON

Deir el Bahari 86. More close-ups of the Osiride Figures. Shadow of the author and photographer is in the foreground.

HATSHEPSUT'S TEMPLE AT DEIR EL BAHARI

13. EGYPT EXPLORATION FUND. THE EXCAVATION OF THE TEMPLE OF QUEEN HATASU AT DEIR-EL-BAHARI. *The Academy* 45 No. 1137 (February 17, 1894: 153-154).

Luxor: Jan. 10, 1894.

Those who revisit Luxor this winter will see a great change in progress at Deir-el-Bahari. Ever since Mariette opened out the now famous bas-relief of Queen Hatasu's expedition to the land of Punt, her singular temple has attracted all lovers of the best Egyptian art. Nothing more exquisite has survived from the great period of the XVIIIth Dynasty than these wall-pictures of ships bringing apes and incense, tusks and skins and precious metals for the queen; and the view of the terrace which is backed by this relief is alone worth a much longer pilgrimage than the visitor must make to Deir-el-Bahari. It has been known that this Terrace and the south end of that above it (which alone used to be accessible) constitute only one corner of the whole temple: vast mounds of rubbish, in certain places between thirty and forty feet high, rose over all the northern part of the terraces, burying far more than Mariette had disclosed, while smaller heaps buried less deeply along the eastern side. Fragments of sculpture, projecting here and there from the mounds, proved that many bas-reliefs must exist beside those laid bare by Mariette, and excited for many years' vain regrets that so much of the work of Hatasu's sculptors should remain unseen. The necessity of banking up the sliding mountain side and cutting through forty feet of earth and stones had been sufficient to deter all explorers until a year ago, when, at last, the committee of the Egypt Exploration Fund determined to carry through what no private excavator could undertake, and made application to the Director-General of Antiquities in Egypt. The concession was accorded readily, accompanied by the offer of the gratuitous loan of plant necessary for excavation on a large scale; but it was stipulated that the temple must be completely *deblaye*, and it was on that understanding that M. Naville began work in January 1893.

Deir el Bahari 87. Broken statues showing their feet section but also where they were positioned on the Upper Terrace before the Upper Colonnade pillars.

HATSHEPSUT'S TEMPLE AT DEIR EL BAHARI

The remarkable results of the first short season have been made public already. Beginning with the uppermost terrace, the excavators found under the *debris* of the cliff an unsuspected group of chambers. Against the western rock was a Hall of Offerings built by the Queen, whose portrait appears there, as elsewhere on the temple, in male guise, accompanied by Thothmes II and III. Adjoining on the east was found a chamber with vestibule, containing a High Altar, built of white stone, and dedicated by the queen to Harmachis. In its possession of this altar, perfectly preserved, with its graduated incline ascending to the platform, Hatasu's Temple is unique among all the Temples of Egypt. Leading into the northern cliff is also a little chapel, a veritable gem of Egyptian painting, dedicated to Thothmes I, his wife, and his mother, Senseneb. Mr. H. Carter, one of the artists attached this year to the expedition, is reproducing the painted reliefs in this shrine, which vie in interest with the Punt sculptures, in color. A little space was cleared also above the colonnade of the second terrace, and other remarkable objects brought to light – namely, two ebony panels, one the side of a shrine about six feet high, dedicated to Amen by Thothmes II, the other part of one of the doors. Both are now at Ghizeh.

The labors of the first season and of the three weeks, which have elapsed since work was recommenced in the second, have produced an astonishing change in the temple. It is literally being cut out of the mountain. When the vast mounds upon the middle terrace have been cleared away – a labor, which cannot proceed very fast - the brilliantly white colonnade round its northwestern end will become a landmark visible for miles. The clearance of this part of the temple will have a double interest: firstly, architecturally, for Mariette's plan has been found to bear very little relation to fact, and the present appearance of the walls promises unusual features of construction; secondly, artistic, for we have found that a wall of unknown painted reliefs exists below the accumulated rubbish. These will be laid bare during the next fortnight; but the main mass of the mounds will hardly disappear this season. Already upon the upper terrace are piled more than 300 sculptured blocks, taken by

FREDERICK MONDERSON

the Copts from all parts of the Temple to build their convent walls. In the mounds of the middle terrace, we shall recover nearly as many more, of which some show already. When all is cleared, and the possibilities of further discovery exhausted, these blocks will be sorted, and, if possible, built up in their original places. This work, which will be supervised by Mr. J. Newberry, the architect attached to the expedition, will be of the first importance both on artistic and historical grounds; for it will result in the reconstruction of several scenes hardly inferior, either in interest or workmanship, to the famous Punt reliefs. For example, much has been recovered of the decoration of the third or lowest terrace, showing that there was represented another nautical scene – the transportation of two obelisks from Elephantine, at the bidding of the Queen. Either in the mounds, or by the demolition of the Coptic walls left standing on the upper terrace, it is hoped that the rest of this scene may be found. Every effort is being made to preserve all evidence as to the subsequent history of the temple, and to find the small objects of antiquity scattered among the *debris*. So far, the main finds of the latter class have been beads, scarabs, and figurines, made of the famous blue-glazed ware. Good Demotic and Coptic *Ostraka* are frequent, and there is much refuse from rifled mummy pits of the XXIInd Dynasty. Some coffins and mummies have been found lying loose among the upper layers of *debris*: one fine case belonged to Namen-Kenkhet-amen, a relative of Osorkhon II and Takelothis; another contains a very finely rolled mummy, for whose reception it was not originally intended; a third is early Coptic, and shows on the front of the outer cloth representations of wine and corn in the hands, while below is the sacred boat of Osiris and over the heart a swastika.

HATSHEPSUT'S TEMPLE AT DEIR EL BAHARI

Deir el Bahari 88. Evidence of how the statues were arranged before the Colonnade.

FREDERICK MONDERSON

The uppermost layer of the mounds consists entirely of the *debris* of previous excavators, who searched either in the temple precinct or immediately above on the hillside for mummy-pits. It contains mummy refuse and many sculptured blocks, but naturally no small objects except those broken or despised by earlier diggers. Several scraps of newspaper, French and German, have been found in it. Below this lies a layer from three to six feet deep of Coptic rubbish, left by the monks of the convent. Here are found *Ostraca* and large quantities of broken blue glaze ware. Immediately below, in the only place on the middle terrace where we have sounded to the bottom, we have found the original pavement. Only, therefore, if we come upon untouched mummy-pits below this pavement, can we hope for any considerable find of small antiquities; for, so far as we have yet seen, there is no *debris* older than Coptic. It is possible that towards the center of the terrace we may find accumulations left untouched by the monks. But, unless such proves to be case, the same methods of excavation need not be resorted to, nor can the same finds be expected; on sites covered with the slowly gathered silt of ages, or in cemeteries lost in the sand.

While the upper stratum of the mounds is being cut away, progress can be made in the copying of the inscriptions, a large number of which, having been pretty thoroughly erased, and present great difficulties. The reconstruction of the Great Altar is to be begun as soon as the masons, now at work on the house, which is being built for the excavators, are free. When the whole site has been cleared, the very costly and difficult work of reconstruction must be begun. That of the western-most wall will present peculiar difficulties, but, from the point of view of artistic effect, will best repay labor and cost. If the stone-slide of the cliff can be banked up, and the present Coptic constructions demolished, a large number of sculptured blocks, belonging to other parts of the temple, will be recovered, and the niches restored to their former beauty. The immense task of cutting away the mounds on the middle terrace will take two seasons at least, and the more shallow accumulation on the lowest terrace will still remain. No excavation of the same magnitude is being conducted at present in Egypt; and it is satisfactory that,

HATSHEPSUT'S TEMPLE AT DEIR EL BAHARI

where so much labor and money must be expended, the monument to be laid bare should be of such exceptional interest. Architecturally, Hatasu's Temple has no parallel: in the quality and preservation of its painted reliefs, it vies with any of the best known tombs; it is placed in a grander situation than any other building in Egypt. The boon which its clearance will confer on lovers of art and the picturesque can hardly be overstated; and science will gain not less by the exploration of a monument of the great XVIIIth Dynasty, the finest existing memorial of Egypt's most famous queen.
D. G. HOGARTH.

Deir el Bahari 89. Head of the Queen as it appeared on one of the statues.

FREDERICK MONDERSON

Deir el Bahari 90. Another head of the Queen, wearing the Double Crown and uraeus now removed from the forehead.

14. EGYPT EXPLORATION FUND: THE TEMPLE OF HATASU AT DEIR EL-BAHARI. *The Academy* 45 No. 1144 (April 7, 1894: 293-294).

Luxor: March 16, 1894.

Ramadan and the hot weather have begun simultaneously; so, the last wages were paid yesterday, the railway was taken up and stored, and all made safe for the summer season.

My forecast, published in a former letter, has proved fairly accurate; we have not been able to clear away entirely the huge mounds on the central terrace, but we have reduced their height everywhere by twenty feet, and on the western and northern side of the terrace have cut them away to the level of the pavement and rock. In the process

HATSHEPSUT'S TEMPLE AT DEIR EL BAHARI

of removing the upper slice, some hundreds of Ostraka, demotic and Coptic were found, besides more Gnostic (?) mummies similar to one mentioned in my former letter. Among the Ostraka there appears to be parts of a library catalogue; but the great majority are letters and legal documents. Only one Greek potsherd has turned up, inscribed with moral reflections, headed .... On the northern side of the terrace, we have laid-open in its entirety a fine colonnade, formerly buried under fallen mountain debris, and it now presents a very fine appearance. It has fifteen sixteen-sided columns, each fourteen feet eight inches high to the top of the abaci. A sandstone architrave rests only on the eight westernmost, and it appears certain that the eastern part of the structure was never finished. A wall of brilliantly white limestone is built against the mountain behind, and four vaulted chapels, un-inscribed and perhaps unfinished, open out of it. Between and inside the columns exist at present a number of mud-brick chambers, which, when excavated, yielded Ramesside pottery and fragments of hieratic papyri, besides scarabs, beads, amulets, and bits of bronze. Neither Ostraka nor any Coptic remains were found in them. These chambers are evidently of an earlier period, and possibly were dwellings of workmen of Rameses II, engaged in a restoration of the temple, and were never destroyed because the completion of this colonnade was not carried through. We have cleared also the hypostyle hall at the western end, which was entered by Mariette, but left full of rubbish. It is one of the best-preserved remains of antiquity in Egypt. The star-spangled ceiling rests on twelve sixteen-sided columns, over fifteen feet high: right and left are brightly-painted funerary niches, and the main walls show scenes still brilliant in coloring, the Queen and Thothmes III offering to gods of the dead. A short staircase ascends at the back of the hall to a three-roomed chapel, on whose walls the Queen offers to Amen Ra and Anubis. As this hall is completely covered in, there is good hope that its paintings may be long preserved with their freshness little if at all impaired.

FREDERICK MONDERSON

Deir el Bahari 91. Visitor takes photo of the Guard on the Upper Terrace.

HATSHEPSUT'S TEMPLE AT DEIR EL BAHARI

South of this hypostyle, and west of the main court of the central terrace, is a portico corresponding in everything but excellence of workmanship, to the famous Punt portico on the south side of the central causeway. It is very much ruined; the square pillars are only complete at the broken end and very few of the architrave blocks or roofing slates are in position. The number of these fallen masses of stone proved a great impediment to us, and we have been able this season only to clear the space between the western rank of pillars and the wall. By so doing we have laid bare a very interesting series of representations, concerning the preliminaries and circumstances of the birth of the Queen. Her mother, Ahmes, appears, conducted by several divinities to the presence of Amen, and the god appears to her in the guise of her husband Thothmes I, as in those well-known scenes in the Luxor Temple, relating to the birth of Amenhotep III. Much restoration has been done on this wall by Rameses II; but the fine portraits of Ahmes herself have escaped his hand, and remain admirable examples of XVIIIth Dynasty art, both in molding and coloring. The inscriptions, though defaced, are fairly legible. Among the debris, which has lain since an early period on the court bounded by this portico, the hypostyle, and the colonnade, we have found most of our small objects of art in stone, ware, or paste. Not much statuary has been discovered; the best piece is the lower half of a kneeling statue of Senmut, the architect of the temple; and a very fine portrait head in sycamore wood, on a part of a mummy case, is worthy of special mention. Amulets, figurines, rings, and scarabs, inscribed and un-inscribed, have been discovered in considerable numbers; and in addition to countless separate beads, some fine necklaces of blue ware, still strung, with pendants attached, were found in the lowest layer of deposit. Papyrus has been unearthed, only in innumerable small fragments; the largest pieces have formed part of copies of the Book of the Dead.

The Temple at Deir el Bahari, as has been often remarked, is not built on a general plan, comparable to that of any other Egyptian temple. Several parts of it, however, taken by them, recall the conventional arrangement of peristyle court, hypostyle, and sanctuary. In fact, Deir el Bahari may be regarded as an aggregate of small temple units. So, on the central terrace we have the northern colonnade, answering to the usual peristyle, which leads to a hypostyle, out of which open a sanctuary. As Thothmes I and II do not appear in any part of it, but only, Hatasu and Thothmes III associated, we may assume that it was built after the death of Thothmes II and before the Queen-regent's rupture with her nephew, and was intended to be more particularly the funerary shrine of Hatasu herself and Thothmes III. It is apparent, however, that the original construction has been altered in this region, and we must wait until the whole terrace has been excavated before we can draw conclusions as to the architectural history of this part of the temple.

Deir el Bahari 92. View of the ruins of the 11th Dynasty temple of Mentuhotep II.

HATSHEPSUT'S TEMPLE AT DEIR EL BAHARI

Deir el Bahari 93. Close-up of the bust of a remaining Osiride Figure of the Queen on the Upper Terrace before the Upper Colonnade.

Mr. John E. Newberry has carried out the reconstruction of the high altar of Harmachis on the upper terrace successfully, nearly all the

FREDERICK MONDERSON

missing parts of the inscription having been found among the debris close at hand. The funerary chapel of Thothmes I has been restored; and in digging out the space between the broken north wall of the altar chamber and the rock face we have found all the missing blocks belonging to a brilliantly painted niche in the vestibule, and from them reconstructed it. Here (for once) Queen Hatasu appears in her male guise un-erased. The broken northern and western main walls have been built up again in part, to be completed if possible next season; and the crumbling cliff above has been shored up strongly with rough masonry. The northern end of the terrace is therefore nearly finished, and the main work of next season must be the reconstruction of the niches in the west wall of the main hall of the upper terrace. The major part of the existing wall about them is of Coptic construction, and must be pulled down, in order that numerous sculptures, belonging to other walls in the temple, may be recovered; but in order that this may be done and the safety of the niches assured, the sliding cliff on the west must be shored up not less strongly than on the north, at great expense of money, time, and labor.

The artists have completed their plates of the Altar Chamber, the Hall of Offerings, and the Chapel of Thothmes I; and these, together with drawings of the altar and the doors of the ebony shrine, discovered last season, will constitute the first fascicule of the complete publication of Deir el Bahari, proposed by the committee of the Fund. It is hoped also that, when the excavation is complete, it will be possible to deduce results bearing generally on Egyptian art. The quantity of relief-work of admirable quality, the variety and freshness of coloring, and the comprehensive find of objects in blue ware ought to afford material or valuable chapters on plastic, pictorial, and ceramic art in the period of the XVIIIth Dynasty. D.G. HOGARTH.

HATSHEPSUT'S TEMPLE AT DEIR EL BAHARI

Deir el Bahari 94. Head of the Queen wearing the White Crown and holding symbols of her power as Pharaoh and sporting a beard.

15. "THE ROYAL MUMMIES OF DEIR-E L-BAHARI." *The Academy* 35 No. 891 (June 1, 1889: 383-384).

Prof Maspero's forthcoming work contains many surprises for those who are interested in the oft-told tale of the royal mummies. Up to the present time, our sole sources of authentic information on this subject have been (1) Prof. Maspero's *compte-rendu* presented to

FREDERICK MONDERSON

the *Academie des Inscriptions* in July, 1881; (2) his paper addressed to the Orientalist Congress of Berlin in 1881 [The Academy, September 17, 1881.]; (3) his essay entitled *La Trouvaille de Deir-el-Bahari*, illustrated by Herr Brugsch's admirable series of photographs, published in 1881; (4) his process-verbal on the un-bandaging of certain Pharaohs in the Boulak Museum of June 1 and 9, 1886 [Reprinted verbatim in the academy from Prof. Maspero's original MS., July 3, and July 31, 1886.]; and a few scattered articles in the pages of the Zeitschrift and the Recueil de Travaux. All these will now be superseded by *Les Mommies Royales de Deir-el-Bahari*, which not only contains a mass of new, important, and interesting matter, but also corrects many errors due to the enforced haste under which the previous reports were written.

When the mummies were transported from Thebes to Boulak, they were temporarily housed in one of the halls of the old museum. The confusion at first was great. Some mummies were not yet identified, while others were in mummy-cases manifestly not their own. Some mummy-cases were without mummies. Some mummies were without mummy-cases; while in more than one instance, a single mummy-case was found to contain two occupants. Whether this disorder was due to the carelessness with which the royal dead had been replaced when their outer wrappings were renewed and their "funerary furniture" repaired by the tomb inspectors of ancient times; or whether it was the Sacrilegious work of the family of Arab plunderers who for years had held the secret of the Deir-el-Bahari vault, who should say? In either case, all that could then and there be done was to classify these various personages according to the inscriptions entered on the mummy-cases in which they were found. These inscriptions were of various dates, some being as originally painted; others altered to suit the occupant of a second-hand coffin; and others written with the pen by XXIst Dynasty scribes, recording the dates of certain official visits of inspection performed during the pontificates of Her-Hor and his successors. To preserve his Mummied royalties from decay or damage being obviously of more importance than to catalogue them with precision Prof. Maspero decided not to un-bandage them till he had provided them with glass

HATSHEPSUT'S TEMPLE AT DEIR EL BAHARI

cases; and the low condition of the Khedivial treasury is curiously illustrated by the fact that it took nearly five years of "patience and economy" to achieve the said cases, which were not completed till the month of April, 1886.

Deir el Bahari 95. More heads, broken statues and a visitor taking a breather.

It was during the summer of 1886 that Prof. Maspero resigned his Egyptian appointment; and the opening of the royal mummies closed his official labors. On June 1, in the presence of the Khedive and a select company of Egyptian and foreign notabilities, the mummies of Rameses II (XIXth Dynasty) and Rameses III (XXth

FREDERICK MONDERSON

Dynasty) were formally un-bandaged. Next followed, on June 9 the un-bandaging of Sekenen-Ra (XVIIth Dynasty) and Ahmes 1 (XVIIIth Dynasty); and subsequently, during the interval which elapsed between the arrival of M. Grebaut and the departure of Prof. Maspero, the rest of the Deir-el-Bahari Pharaohs, with the single exception of Amenhotep I, were duly opened. Each body in succession was carefully unwrapped and measured by Prof. Maspero, M. Bouriant, M. Insinger, and Dr. Fouquet, assisted by M. Mathey in the capacity of chemical analyst. These measurements, which are calculated on the French metrical system, give the lengths of the hand, foot, arm, forearm, etc.; various diameters of the skull; the circumference of head, shoulders, and waist; the length of the orbit of the eye, and the distance between the two orbits; the width of the mouth, length of nose and chin, circumference of pelvis, facial angle, etc. etc.; all having been twice taken and verified. Even the position of the orifice of the ear has been noted, and one learns with no little interest that, in at least one instance – e.g., that of the Princess Sit-Kames - this orifice is parallel with the root of the nose and somewhat above the line of the eye, precisely as we see it represented in Egyptian statuary.

Deir el Bahari 96. Upper portions of three remaining Osiride Figures with pillar up- front and "Proto-Doric" column in the rear on the Upper Terrace as part of the Upper Colonnade.

HATSHEPSUT'S TEMPLE AT DEIR EL BAHARI

The results of this prolonged scientific investigation have more than justified the five years' delay. A rich harvest of physiological observations has been reaped; a new Pharaoh has been identified; some important lacunae in the history of the XVIIth and XXIst Dynasties have been more or less filled up; several papyri and some beautiful specimens of ancient Egyptian jewelry have been found on certain mummies; and some royal personages, who were at first misnamed are restored to their place in history. Thus, the mummy contained in the gigantic mummy-case of queen Aah-hotep turns out to be King Pinotem I; and he, with the shaven head and Voltaire face, whom we have hitherto accepted as Pinotem I, is more than conjecturally identified by Prof. Maspero with Thothmes I. So also, one of two mummies found in the mummy-case of Princess Nesikhonsu proves, to be a king whose winding-sheet is inscribed with a couple of lines of hieratic writing, thus translated: "Expedition made to the Abode, in the year VII, to enwrap the King Ra Kha-em-uas" - the "Abode" being evidently the "eternal abode of Amenhotep," which, in the time of the priest-kings, was used as a place of refuge for the earlier Pharaohs, and is thus mentioned in one of the official entries scribbled on the coffin of Rameses II. The King Ra Kha-em-uas, whose name, at all events in this form, is unknown, is identified by Prof. Maspero with Rameses XII, the contemporary and predecessor of Her-Hor, and by M. Grebaut, with Rameses IX. Among other genealogical emendations, Prof. Maspero makes out Queen Aah-hotep (the famous Queen Aah-hotep of the Boulak jewels) to be the wife, not of Kames, as hitherto believed, but of Sekenen-Re, and the mother of both Kames and Ahmes I. He also, with infinite skill, based on an exhaustive study of a vast number of scattered inscriptions, reconstructs the framework of the XXIst Dynasty - thus, for the first time, presenting a satisfactory solution of one of the most difficult problems in Egyptian history. Still more interesting, because entirely new, is his chapter on "The Principality of Thebes under the last Descendants of the Priest-Kings," in which he traces the boundaries of this sacerdotal and military fief, the history of its vicissitudes under the

FREDERICK MONDERSON

XXIInd, XXIst, and, XIXth Dynasties, and the final abolition of the office of High Priest of Amen in the time of Piankhi.

Deir el Bahari 97. Close-up of three of the Osiride Figures wearing the Double Crown.

Many details, now for the first time made public respecting certain of the mummies, are extremely curious. The last toilette of some royal ladies of the XXIst Dynasty was, for instance, most elaborate, the wrinkles caused by the process of mummification being filled up with some kind of enamel, **the skin colored with ochre**, the cheeks and lips rouged, and false eyes introduced under the shriveled and half-open lids; thus, giving a horribly life-like appearance to the faces, as shown in the auto-type illustrations from Herr Brugsch's photographs. Others, though now quite bare of ornaments, had evidently been buried in all their jewels, like Queen Aah-hotep; necklaces, diadems and bracelets having left their impress on the withered skin. Dr. Fouquet and M. Mathey have mummified many in contorted attitudes, as if they had died in convulsions; but the ghastliest interest of all attaches to the remains of an anonymous prince, who appears to have been embalmed alive, and upon whose mummy reports are furnished. The brain, heart, stomach, etc., of this unfortunate man are intact, as in life. The body was found tightly bound in three places, namely, round the shoulders, round the wrists and loins, and round the feet; these

HATSHEPSUT'S TEMPLE AT DEIR EL BAHARI

ligatures being drawn with such force as to leave deep furrows in the flesh. This done, he appears to have been covered with a thick coat of bitumen, lime, and pounded resin, and to have been enwound from head to foot with bandages soaked in some glutinous preparation which caused them to adhere with such tenacity that they had to be sawn off. The expression of the face, the open mouth, the swollen and knotted muscles, bear witness to his desperate struggles, and to the horrors of his last agony. His age was about twenty-three, and in his ears were small gold earrings. That he was a personage of high rank, and the victim of some unspeakable tragedy, admits of no doubt; but to his name and parentage, and to the circumstances of his fate, no clue remains.

Deir el Bahari 98. A tremendous balancing act but also indicative of how architraves cover distances. Notice the cut stone rests directly in the middle of the two columns. This is joined by additional slabs positioned on columns set right and left and thus the distance is covered.

Want of space forbids me to indulge in more gleanings from Prof. Maspero's deep series of uniform excellence which reflects the highest honor on the French school of Egyptology, but which, being addressed to specialists rather than to the public, has neither achieved, nor is intended to achieve, popularity. If, however, I am not greatly mistaken, Prof. Maspero's new contribution is predestined to such a sale as has been heretofore unknown in the history of the series. It will be eagerly bought and read by thousands to whom big scientific arguments will probably be caviare, but who will be enthralled by big matter and fascinated by big style. AMELIA B. EDWARDS.

Deir el Bahari 99. Entrance into the Upper Court with its Peristyle Colonnade as visitors mill around in the heart of the Temple.

Deir el Bahari 100. The double of row of "Proto-Doric" columns, against the eastern wall of the Upper Court, with the southern wall and gated opening to the south.

HATSHEPSUT'S TEMPLE AT DEIR EL BAHARI

Deir el Bahari 101. Another view of the Courts, its columns, people milling around and the retaining wall against the mountain as a backdrop.

16. "THE DAHR-EL-BAHARI MUMMIES."
The Academy 38 No. 955 (August 23, 1890: 157-58).

St. Leonard's, Malvern Link: August 18, 1890.

So much has been written about the state of the Dayr-el-Bahari mummies in the GI Museum, and of their probable decay if they remain in their present resting place, that it is only fair that English people should be made acquainted with the report on their condition drawn up a few weeks ago by Dr. Fouquet at the request of M. Grebaut, and published in the *Journal Officiel of the Egyptian Government*.

M. Grebaut begged Dr. Fouquet to examine the mummies and report on the following queries:
(1) Whether the mummy of Seti I developed signs of decay since it was unrolled from its bandages.
(2) Whether the efflorescence observed on certain parts of the skin of this mummy the result of damp.
(3) Whether this mummy in particular, more generally all the mummies in the museum were threatened with destruction.

FREDERICK MONDERSON

Now Dr. Fouquet is singularly qualified to give an opinion on these points, as he was the medical man called in to make the anthropometrical measurements of these royal persons when they were first unrolled in June, 1886.

The following is a resume of his answers to Mr. Grebaut's queries:

(1) Already on June 16, 1886, when the mummy of Seti I was unbandaged, we observed an efflorescence on various parts of the body (on the chest, ribs, toes, etc.), where it may still be seen.
(2) A portion of this efflorescence has been removed, and has been placed in two bottles. One was kept at the museum; the other been handed to Dr. Fouquet for microscopic examination. The result of this examination was to show that it was composed of scales and prisms of crystallized salts, and in no way could its formation be attributed to the effect of damp. ("Ni mycetium ni spores" are Dr. Fouquet's words.) It was, in fact the result of the salts employed in the embalming of the mummy, and of the bitumen used at a later date to repair the damage done to the body when it was removed from its original resting-place to Dayr-el-Bahari. Dr. Fouquet further remarks: "Cette matiere ne s'est formee que lentement dans le cours des siecles."
(3) To satisfy those who assert that mummies are rapidly decomposing in the atmosphere of the Ghizeh Museum, Dr. Fouquet made several experiments to induce the growth and spread of mold (taken off paste and old cheese) on fragments of mummy and mummy cloth exposed to damp. Such experiments resulted uniformly in sterility.

I have Dr. Fouquet's entire report in French before me, with its careful chemical analysis of the salts in question. It will be a great relief to all Egyptologists if the previous rumors circulated as to the condition of the mummies can be proved to be without ground.

M.L. Herbert McClure, Member of the Committee of the Egyptian Exploration Fund, and Hon. Local Secretary for S.W.; Member of the Society for the Preservation of Ancient Monuments in Egypt.

HATSHEPSUT'S TEMPLE AT DEIR EL BAHARI

Deir el Bahari 102. Upper Court from the East. Double row of columns, Portico to Sanctuary, Niches, Northern and Western Walls and the mountain as a backdrop.

17. "THE DAHR-EL-BAHARI MUMMIES."
The Academy 38 No. 956 (August 30, 1890: 179-180).

London: August 25, 1890.

In reference to the very interesting communication from Mr. Herbert McClure, respecting the Dayr-el-Bahari mummies now in the Ghizeh Museum, I venture to make a few observations.

Mr. McClure informs us that portions of the efflorescence had been submitted to Dr. Fouquet at the request of M. Grebaut for microscopic examination and analysis, the result being that the matter was found to consist of thin scales and prisms of crystallized salts, but the particular salts were not mentioned.

FREDERICK MONDERSON

Now it would be interesting to know whether the substance referred to was natron - that is, carbonate of soda. It is well known that, previous to the process of embalming, the body of the deceased was steeped in natron for seventy days. The object of this immersion seems to have been to dissolve the tissues and so leave little but skin and bone. The space occupied by the flesh was filled during the process of embalming by bitumen and various spices, the body having been previously washed, doubtless in order to remove the organic matter dissolved by the alkaline solution. Traces of the salt would probably remain, and hence the appearance of the efflorescence, which, though originally locked up by the bitumen, would, in the process of desiccation during many centuries, eventually find its way to the surface. It is probable that the mummies have gone through this process long anterior to their removal from the tomb, and the appearance of the salt now does not seem to justify any fears for their stability under the present conditions.

As regards the risk of exposure to damp, the mummies are safer when housed in the Ghizeh Museum than they could have been at Bulaq, where they would have been exposed not only to the effluvia from the river, but also to the moisture which, during high Nile, percolates through the banks.

It is satisfactory to learn that, on the authority of so able and experienced a scientist as Dr. Fouquet, the efflorescence is declared to be entirely inorganic in its nature, and not the result of any mold or fungoid growth.

As to the final disposal of these wonderful and impressive relics of the past, I may be permitted to ask whether, the laudable curiosity of the learned and a large number of the cultured classes having been gratified, it would not be more in accordance with respect for the dead if they could be once more sealed up-and reverently restored to their tomb? FRANK DILLON

HATSHEPSUT'S TEMPLE AT DEIR EL BAHARI

Deir el Bahari 103. Mr. Jackson strolls in the Upper Court during his explorations, as other visitors mill around.

18. EGYPT EXPLORATION FUND: "THE EXPLORATION OF DER EL BAHARI." Luxor: Jan. 18, 1895. *The Academy* 47 No. 1188 (February 9, 1895: 133).

THE clearing of the Funerary Temple of Queen Hatshepsu, which has been in process during two winter seasons past, was resumed at the beginning of December, and has been prosecuted without intermission. Readers of the Academy will remember that, when heat and Ramadan interrupted the work last March, the upper of the three Terraces or Platforms was left almost clear, and the huge mounds upon the North Court of the Central Terrace had been cut away round the north and west sides, and much diminished in all

FREDERICK MONDERSON

parts, but still a great mass of earth and chips and all kinds of debris from twenty to twenty-five feet high encumbered two-thirds of the Court, while the South Court of the same Terrace, the Third or Lower Terrace, and some chambers on the south of the Upper Terrace, had not been touched at all.

The chief result of the past weeks has been the complete and final clearance of the great mounds from the North Court, down to its pavement, where it exists, or the native rock where the pavement has been ripped away or was never laid. At the smallest computation, over 42,000 cubic meters of rubbish have been removed from this Court alone, and shot at a distance of a quarter of a mile; and the result is a complete transformation of the site, and a remarkable change in the view obtained of the Deir el Bahari valley, when approached from Sheikh Abdul Gurneh, or as seen across the Nile from distant Luxor. The brilliantly white columns of the Northern Colonnade and Hypostyle, and the walls of the North and South Porticoes, no longer masked by the mounds, show boldly upon the yellow background of the Libyan cliffs; and the Funerary Temple of the XVIIIth Dynasty takes once more as conspicuous a place in the Theban landscape as the Memnonia, of the XIXth and XXth Dynasties.

The further exploration of the North Court has served to confirm a theory, suggested last year that this part of the temple was latest built and never finished. The name of Thothmes III alone appears beside the Queen's in the Hypostyle; and it is therefore most probable that she designed this "wing" to serve someday as the funerary chapel of her ward, but when the latter grew to man's estate, and the strife which is supposed to have ensued between himself and his guardian became acute (or possibly on the Queen's death), the building was arrested and never taken in hand again, except for one abortive moment in Ptolemaic times. The court before the Hypostyle is unpaved, and the rock only roughly leveled. But half-way across it, as one proceeds towards the causeway, pavement begins to be seen at a level slightly lower than the unfinished rock surface; and upon this pavement lay a great pyramid of clean limestone chips, which

HATSHEPSUT'S TEMPLE AT DEIR EL BAHARI

here and there an un-worked block of quarry stone, which seems to have been left by the masons of Hatshepsu, when their work was stopped. Over this pyramid and sloping down to the pavement near the causeway is a layer of finer disintegrated stuff, fallen from the mountain. This represents the centuries immediately following Hatshepsu, when her unfinished temple came to be used as a cemetery; and we have found in it, buried as deep as possible in the light limestone deposit, and sometimes right on the pavement, some good Saite coffins, intact with their mummified occupants. A group of mummies - father, mother, and child - laid together in the rock, is of unusual interest, because the ornamentation of their wrappings is of the Gnostic type, found here last year, and the wooden name-label, still firmly attached to the breast of the man, places the Coptic character of this type of burial beyond doubt. The writing on the label is not of an early period, perhaps not earlier than the fifth century A.D. The next layer above this belongs to a much later period, when this abode of the dead was once more taken possession of by the living, in the early Coptic epoch. Here we have burnt stuff of every kind, densely packed shards, straw, and miscellaneous rubbish; and, with the interruption now and again of another stratum of mountain debris, brought down by some great fall, the Coptic layers repeated themselves almost up to the summit of the mound, as we found it at first; but the actual crown was debris of the cliff, fallen since the destitution of the Coptic convent. The Coptic strata have yielded us this season, as last, a find of Ostraka, to the number of several hundred, Coptic and demotic from above, a few hieratic from below; and, also, infinite scraps of papyrus, beads, and other remnants of earlier burials disturbed by the Copts or by diggers.

But only between the pyramid of masons' chips and the Colonnade on the still unfinished rock floor have we found scarabs and other small antiques, not proceeding from disturbed burials: for that side of the Court alone was open for passage, while the temple was still used for worship. This season we have recovered some 200 inscribed scarabs, and twice that number uninscribed, together with many amulets and countless beads from so much of the Court as

FREDERICK MONDERSON

was left to be dug north of the pavement-edge. Some of these scarabs and scarabeoids present very unusual forms, and are of admirable color and workmanship. Fragments of statuary, small objects in wood, and a few bits of bronze remain to be added to the list.

The central Causeway has been cleared, and found to be in very ruinous condition. To judge from sculptured fragments lying near it, it appears to have been decorated in part with a frieze of crowned hawks and uraei, similar to, but smaller than, those on the southern confining wall of the temple. No trace has been seen yet of the staircases with which Mariette breaks the Causeway in his plan.

Immediately to the north of the Causeway, where neither the fall from the mountain nor the masons' chips blocked the Court, the Copts seem to have shot the main part of their rubbish; and here we have found countless broken remains of important Saite burials, and some relics of Hatshepsut's own period more noteworthy than ordinary-for example, large fragments of a good stele bearing the cartouche of Thothmes IIII, and erected by a priest of Hathor and Amen in the temple, and pieces of very fine blue ware. In the southwest angle of the Court occurs an unexpected architectural puzzle: a double line of square columns, made up of fragments of older work, erased and resculptured, trends north-eastward at an acute angle to the Causeway. It is out of line or symmetry with everything else in the temple, and evidently of later date, though not post-Pharaonic; but why anyone should have undertaken the labor of piling these massy fragments one on the other, in order to erect a roof over this corner of the Court, is not readily apparent. It is just possible that a rude chapel was built here, on account of some important grave dug hard by in late Pharaonic times; and we shall have to search carefully all this corner of the Court.

HATSHEPSUT'S TEMPLE AT DEIR EL BAHARI

Deir el Bahari 104. From the southeast in the Upper Court, view of bases of broken "Proto-Doric" columns of the Peristyle Colonnade. Visitors are admiring the Portico to the Sanctuary against the retaining wall of the mountain.

Furthermore, some progress has been made with the clearance of certain small chambers on the south of the Upper Terrace, but this work cannot be finished until their walls are shored up for, they are in very ruinous condition, and held up in part by the rubbish inside and out. Careful exploration has been prosecuted also outside the southern limits of the temple, as indicated on all the plans, in order to determine whether these are the true limits; but except for a short terrace-chamber above the Hathor Shrine, no extension southward has been found.

The vestibule of the Hathor Shrine (Mariette's "Speos du Sud") has been cleared in part and will be completed at once; then the South Court of the Central Terrace will be taken in hand. Except where Mariette has thrown the debris, which he dug out of the Punt Portico, there is but little depth of deposit upon this part of the temple, and it will not take long to clear. The Lower Terrace has been disencumbered in part already; and its further clearance will be the last item in this year's program, and, it is hoped, the last heavy piece of work to be done in the Temple. The draughts men, Messrs. H. Carter and Brown, who are copying this year the Northern Hypostyle and Porticoes of the Central Terrace and part of the Southern chambers of the Upper, will require another full season to complete the necessary plates for publication.

Two theories, which have been credited with regard to this temple, still await confirmation. Firstly, was anything ever built on the site at a period earlier than that of Hatshepsu? Two or three bits of sculpture, apparently of the XIth Dynasty, have been found in the mounds, but they come almost without doubt from the early tombs near the temple. We have seen no trace whatever of the small shrine of Mentuhotep II whose remains Mariette says that he detected; and we must conclude that he was misled by tomb-fragments. For the rest, everything in the temple, whether construction or debris is of the Queen's time or later.

Secondly, are the tombs of Hatshepsu and Thothmes attached in any way to the Temple? The analogy of Seti I's shrine of Gurneh, of the Ramesseum, and of Medinet Habu points to a negative conclusion, and we can find no trace in floors, ceilings, or walls of any entrance to a tomb. Nevertheless, the exclusively funerary character of most of Hatshepsut's Temple, and it's strange position against and almost under the cliffs, which are pierced on the other side by the Tombs of the Kings, make it difficult to abandon altogether the idea (strongly credited by the Arabs of the locality) that the unknown tombs of the XVIIIth Dynasty will be found some day near Deir el Bahari. The chances, however, of their entrances being either in or connected with the temple seem very small. Many people before ourselves have pierced the walls of the chambers, and lifted paving-slabs in unsuccessful attempts to find them, and we do not appear to be fated to meet with any better fortune. D. D. Hogarth.

HATSHEPSUT'S TEMPLE AT DEIR EL BAHARI

Deir el Bahari 105. View of the Portico entrance into the "Holy of Holies," Sanctuary, with a modern gate and rope to keep out intruders. To the left and right niches housed statues of various sizes of which only a few remain, broken, but *in situ*.

P.S. I reopen this letter to record the discovery (due to Mr. H. Carter) of several blocks belonging to the ruined south wall of the Punt scenes. We have recovered now the lost King of Punt, and much of the scenery of his land. This find, in view of the admitted excellence of these particular reliefs and the unusual interest attaching to pictures of marsh-dwellings in tropical Africa, may rank among the best results of our work here. D. G. H.

Deir el Bahari 106. Close-up of the granite entrance (left); and lintel overhead at the Sanctuary doorway. Notice both Hatshepsut and Thutmose III, in White Crown (left) and Red Crown (right), kneeling and presenting jars of ointment to the defaced Amon whose feathered crown is still visible.

It is interesting that while Thutmose III damaged and erased much of Hatshepsut's images, he did not touch that of Amon, then the principal god. This particular erasure came later at the hands of Amenhotep IV, Ikhnaton, in his vendetta against Amon wherever his name could be found.

FREDERICK MONDERSON

Deir el Bahari 107. Close up of the two halves of the previous image showing both Hatshepsut and Thutmose III kneeling and making offerings in jars to Amon

19. EGYPT EXPLORATION FUND. "THE EXCAVATIONS AT DEIR EL-BAHARI." *The Academy* 47 No. 1196 (March 16, 1895: 242-243). Deir el Bahari: February 22, 1895.

THE clearing of Deir el-Bahari is drawing towards its end. Not only is the middle platform completely cleared and leveled, but also the retaining wall on the southern side is showing its enormous hawks and traces of the vultures and asps, which have been erased by the enemies of the worship of Amon. Parallel to the retaining wall runs an enclosure wall which did not reach the height of the platform, but which formed with it a passage ending in a staircase, now entirely ruined. It seems to have been the only way to reach the Hathor Shrine.

Among the most interesting discoveries made lately are those alluded to in Mr. Hogarth's letter (*Academy*, February 9) of fragments of the famous Punt wall, found scattered here and there in various parts of the temple. Small as the fragments often are, they

HATSHEPSUT'S TEMPLE AT DEIR EL BAHARI

give us important information as to the nature of the land of Punt. Its African character comes out more and more clearly. Although the name of Punt may have applied also to the coast of South Arabia, it is certain that the Egyptian boats sent by the Queen landed in Africa. In the newly discovered fragments, we find two kinds of monkeys climbing up the palm-trees: the dog-headed baboon, the sacred animal of Thoth; and the rounded-headed monkey. Then we see bulls with long and twisted horns, like the animals, which, as I have been told, were brought to Egypt some years ago from the Abyssinian coast. Two panthers are fighting together; a giraffe is showing its head, which reaches to the top of a tree; and a hippopotamus is also sculptured as one of the animals of the country.

A small fragment speaks of "cutting ebony in great quantity." And on another we see the axes of the Egyptians felling large branches on one of the dark-stemmed trees, which had not hitherto been identified, but which are now proved to be ebony. A small chip shows that the people had two different kinds of houses, one of which was made of wickerwork. It is doubtful whether we shall find much more; unfortunately, what we have is quite insufficient for allowing us to reconstruct the invaluable Punt sculptures, which have been most wantonly destroyed in ancient and modern times.

Deir el Bahari 108. Creative joining of the two faces of the Sanctuary entrance, with the Queen wearing the White Crown to the left and the Red Crown to the right.

Nevertheless, it is Thutmose III's name that appears here and he may have erased the Queen's and inserted his own.

HATSHEPSUT'S TEMPLE AT DEIR EL BAHARI

Deir el Bahari 108a. Decoration above entrance sporting the *Suten Bat* and *Son of Ra* titles, *Men-Kheper-Ra* and *Thutmose III*.

Deir el Bahari 108b. Champollion first named these 16-sided "Proto-Doric" columns, he first observed at Beni Hasan.

FREDERICK MONDERSON

Deir el Bahari 108c and d. Inner reaches and Corbeled ceiling studded with stars against a blue sky.

Deir el Bahari 108e and f. Ceiling and wall decoration in the temple's inner reaches.

HATSHEPSUT'S TEMPLE AT DEIR EL BAHARI

Deir el Bahari 108g and h. Saying hello and goodbye.

On February 1, we at last came upon an untouched mummy-pit in clearing the vestibule of the Hathor shrine. In a place where the slabs of the pavement had been broken, we tried the ground to see if there was anything underneath, as we have done many times without success. On this occasion the workmen soon discovered that there was a pit roughly hewn in the rock, and filled with what they call fine rubbish, *tourab kois*, which means "untouched." When we came to a depth of about 12 feet, we found the bricks and the stones, which closed the entrance to the side chamber. I removed them with my own hands, got into the very narrow opening, and found myself in a small rock-hewn chamber. It was nearly filled with three large wooden coffins placed near each other, of rectangular form, with arched lids, and a post at each of the four corners. On the two nearest the entrance were five wooden hawks, one on each post, and one about the middle of the body. Every coffin had at the feet a wooden jackal, with a long tail hanging along

FREDERICK MONDERSON

the box. Wreaths of flowers were laid on them, and at head and feet stood a box containing a great number of small porcelain ushabtis.

The opening of the chamber being very small, it is evident that these large coffins were taken into the tomb in pieces, and put together afterwards. We undid the one next to the door, and found inside it a second coffin in the form of a mummy, with head and ornaments well painted, and a line of hieroglyphs well down to the feet. We did the same with the two others, and found that they also contained a second coffin, which we hauled up through the opening of the tomb. When we had stored them in our house, we opened the second coffins, and we found in each case a third inside, brilliantly painted with representations of gods and scenes from the Book of the Dead. In this third box was the mummy, very well wrapped in pink cloth, with a net of beads all over her body, a scarab with outspread wings, also made of beads, and the four funeral genii. We unrolled one of the mummies, and then found it carefully wrapped in good clothes, which might be used at the present day as napkins or even handkerchiefs. Over the body was a very hard crust of bitumen: we had to use a chisel to break it. There were no amulets or ornaments of any kind except the beads.

These three mummies, which required nine coffins for their burial, are those of a priest of Monthu, Thotaufankh, his mother and his aunt. They evidently belong to the Saitic epoch, and are among the good specimens of that period. I consider that we were, very fortunate in finding an unrifled tomb. It is clear that, after the XXIInd Dynasty, when the temple was no longer used as a place of worship, it became a vast cemetery. But, when we reflect that even in the middle of the last century people had begun to dig here for mummies, it is astonishing to find that this tomb escaped in an edifice, which has been ransacked during nearly 130 years. EDOUARD NAVILLE.

HATSHEPSUT'S TEMPLE AT DEIR EL BAHARI

Deir el Bahari 109. Visitors strive for that memorable photo of the Sanctuary.

Deir el Bahari 110. Here's a better view of the different sized niches, the remaining statues and the column stumps in the foreground.

20. EGYPT EXPLORATION FUND. "THE EXCAVATIONS AT DEIR EL BAHARI." *The Academy* 47 No 1197 (April 13, 1895: 321-322).

The clearing of the Temple of Deir el Bahari is practically finished. This great work has extended over nearly three winters, and has occupied 215 working days. The Temple of Hatshepsu, as it can be

FREDERICK MONDERSON

seen from the village of Luxor, now presents a striking sight to the traveler coming from Goorneh along the old avenue or sidewise from the Ramesseum. The proto-Doric columns give one the impression of a Greek temple; and the white limestone, of which they are made, though by no means to be compared to white marble, contributes to that illusion.

The very last days of the excavation have been productive of interesting results. In the sanctuary a heavy lintel, thrown down by mummy diggers, nearly closed the entrance from the first chamber to the second. This lintel has been raised, and the door rebuilt. I was thus enabled to clear the first hall of the sanctuary down to the pavement, as well as the two next chambers. In doing so I discovered an interesting piece of sculpture, a great part of which has unfortunately been destroyed by the Copts. It shows the garden of the temple, the ponds of water in the neighborhood, and the fishes, birds, and water-plants living in them. Curiously, these ponds - of which there are four-, are called "the ponds of milk, which are on both sides of this god [Amon] - when he rests in his temple." One may wonder how it was possible to have ponds and a garden it such a desolate place as Deir el Bahari, at a mile distance from the nearest well in the cultivated land. I have not found any traces of the ponds, but I have proofs that vegetation was artificially sustained. On the lower platform there are several pits sunk into the rock to a depth of about ten feet. They are full of Nile mud, hardened by the watering of the palm-trees or the vines planted in them. Several of the stumps were found *in situ*. The natives told me that there are a great number of these pits, which they call *sagyiehs,* along the avenue where the Sphinxes stood. It is not impossible that in old times the Sphinxes couched under the shade of palm trees-and tamarisks, like the rams in front of the Pylons of the temples at Karnak.

An interesting work, which will have to be done next winter, now that the clearing is finished, is the sorting of the inscribed and sculptured stones, and, if possible, replacing them in their original positions. Coptic walls will have to be taken down, as the

HATSHEPSUT'S TEMPLE AT DEIR EL BAHARI

inhabitants of the convent have made the most barbarous use of interesting and fine sculptures. In the first year of the work, I discovered a block belonging to a representation, at present unique, of an obelisk being transported on a large boat. Its foreparts only could be seen. Later on, I found the rudder of the boat, but the middle part was still missing. It has now been found. The obelisk is seen nearly, in its whole length; it is tied to its sledge by a long parallel rope and at regular intervals by, cross-ropes over each of the wedges, on which the heavy monuments rest. Another sculpture, the blocks which have been found in the basement of the Coptic tower, shows a sitting colossus on a boat towed along the river by two barges with many rowers. As we know where this sculpture belongs it will be easy to put it back again.

Where was the tomb of Hatshepsu? is a question that has often been asked. I am now able to point to a place, of which I shall not yet venture to say more than that; it is not improbable that it was her tomb. In the passage of the retaining wall of the middle platform and the enclosure we came upon an inclined plane, cut in the rock and leading to the entrance of a large tomb. The rubbish was untouched; the slope had evidently been made of a large stone coffin. Everything most promising; but when we had passed the entrance, we got into a long sloping shaft reaching nearly under the Hathor Shrine. The shaft ended in a large chamber, in the middle of which lay a quite plain wooden rectangular coffin, containing bones, and bearing only a few hieratic signs. Evidently this tomb had not been made for so poor a burial; and as there were no signs of plundering, the natural conclusion is, that the corpse for which it was destined never was put into it. If we remember the hatred with which Thothmes III pursed his aunt's memory - his efforts not only to wipe away the record of her life, but also even to annihilate her ka, her "double," in the other world - can we suppose that he would have allowed her body to be buried sumptuously in the tomb which she had prepared? Would he not rather have destroyed her body or deprived her of burial? It is, therefore, not impossible that this tomb, discovered in the passage close to the Hathor shrine, was that which Hatshepsu had prepared for herself.

FREDERICK MONDERSON

The day before the date I had fixed for closing the work - while completing the clearing of the same passage - quite unexpectedly the workman came upon a large foundation deposit in a small rock-cut pit, about three feet down. The pit was covered with mats, under which lay first a few pots of common earthenware; afterwards about fifty wooden objects, the models of an implement, the use of which I do not understand, and which we will call for the present winnowers. Each one of them bears the inscription: "the good god Ramaka, the worshipper of Amon el Teren (Deir el Bahari);" then we took out fifty wooden hoes, four bronze slabs, a hatchet, a knife, eight wooden models of adzes, and eight larger adzes with bronze blades; at the bottom ten little pots of alabaster, and also ten little baskets, which I regard as molds for bread. All the wooden or bronze objects, and also the alabaster pots, bear the same inscription. These things have no artistic beauty; there is no precious metal or stone among them; but they are interesting as historical evidence. They are very similar to a set of deposits of Thothmes III, discovered by Mariette at Karnak, and now exhibited in the Ghizeh Museum.

The principal work of next winter will consist in repairing and propping up walls, which would go to ruin, and also in putting in their places all the inscriptions, which we may be able to reconstitute. Hitherto travelers have often left Deir el Bahari unvisited; it is now one of the most interesting sites on the west of Thebes. EDOUARD NAVILLE.

HATSHEPSUT'S TEMPLE AT DEIR EL BAHARI

Deir el Bahari 111. Close-up of the niches with the statues holding ankhs.

21. "THE DER EL BAHARI EXHIBITION." *The Academy* 48 No. 1210 (July 13, 1895: 37).

Not only the inner circle of Egyptologists but the general public will find it well worth their while to pay a visit to Burlington House during the few remaining days that the Der el Bahari Exhibition is to remain open. The objects exhibited at the Society of Antiquaries, coming from the intensely hot soil of the Luxor Desert, display in a singular degree that marvelous preservation which constitutes the main attraction of Egyptian antiquities. Although dating back for the most part to at least 1400 B.C., many of these objects look as though made yesterday, and have all the mysterious charm of things over which decay seems to have no power.

General interest is awakened by the large case on the left of the room, in which are set out a unique series of tools, models, vases, and the like which were marked with Queen Hatshepsut's name ("Good god Ramaka, beloved of Amen in Serui"), and deposited below the foundations of her temple. The mats, which covered them, lie on the center table hard by. The metal blades of the tools

FREDERICK MONDERSON

are of bronze, the handles and wooden objects of sycamore, the latter especially seeming miraculously new, considering that they have been buried about 3500 years. This large deposit, the earliest known, was found last February on the extreme south of the temple in a pit with a small recess scooped out on one side. There are fourteen jars of unglazed red ware; ten pots of alabaster, with original covers; fifty wooden models, probably of threshing-sledges; fifty wooden hoes without the usual cross binding, the leathers for which were found in bundles close by; eight large adzes, with bronze blades and red leather binding, wonderfully preserved; eight small adze-handles without blades; eleven stands of basket-work for jars; four bronze blades; a sacrificial knife and an axe. Five fine blue scarabaeus of the Queen were found nearby. This collection, singular in date, size, and character, is perhaps the most remarkable that has ever found its way to London.

The large painted coffins, which show conspicuously at the sides of the room, are notable chiefly for their preservation and the completeness of all the accessories of burial - the bead-nets, with genii in blue bead-work on the breasts of the dead; the wooden hawks and jackals, symbols of Horus and Anubis, on guard over the coffins; and the wooden boxes filled with blue *ushabti* figurines at the feet. The mummies in them are those of a priest of Khonsu, his mother and her sister; and all were found together in a pit excavated at a later period than the Queen's in a corner of her temple, and preserved inviolate to this day by the collapse of the roof above.

In the showcases are displayed a great variety of smaller objects. In that in the farthest window on the left are scarabs, amulets, etc., of the famous Deir el Bahari blue glaze. The inscribed scarabs of the XVIIIth Dynasty, shown here, amount to over 400. The rarest objects in this case are probably an exquisite green frog with red eyes, and the complete blue vase of Princess Nesikhonsu at the back of the case. In the center of the room, beside Ptolemaic "Canopic" jars and remains of broken up burials of the Saite period, are displayed more specimens of the local blue ware, beads of all kinds, uninscribed scarabs, chessmen, necklaces, and fragments of large vases showing great variety of geometric and floral design. On the

HATSHEPSUT'S TEMPLE AT DEIR EL BAHARI

left side, as one proceeds towards the back of the room, the late Coptic breast-clothe should be noted, one with name-label attached. These are especially interesting as affording clear evidence of a survival of the practice of mummification, with all the ideas it implied, far into Christian times. The bronze objects are not very remarkable; but a few specimens of Coptic Ostraka, selected from over 1000, are of great interest to students of early ritual and church history. One, it may be noted, contains matter bearing with singular appositeness on the controversy as to the remarriage of divorced persons. Much is expected from this enormous find of documents dating from a very early and interesting period of the Coptic Church. A fine coffin-mask in sycamore wood and rare specimens of wooden dovetails for bonding blocks together on the left side, and an artist's trial piece on the right side, ought to be looked at; and on a small table near the door lies a child's coffin with a pair of baby shoes buried with it. The shoes are cut in two to render them useless to a spoiler, while they would remain as good as ever for the child's use in a spirit world: the parents believed that the child would carry and wear its shoes alternately on its ghostly journey, as they carried and wore theirs (and the *fellahin* does still) on earth. Near the coffin lies another small one, containing a rudely cut witch-doll.

The wall opposite to the door is covered with a large collection of drawings for publication; and it should be observed that these represent the main reason for the excavation of Der el Bahari. The fine reliefs, with which the temple walls are covered, have been revealed, many of them for the first time now, and will be reproduced in annual installments. The sculptures, constituting by far the largest class of the finds, can only be represented very imperfectly in such an exhibition as this at Burlington House. In former days they would have been ripped off ruthlessly and brought away; now they are left in position, secured and guarded; and visitors to the exhibition will bear in mind that on that account they do not see the tenth part of what the Der el Bahari excavation has actually brought to light.

Deir el Bahari 111a. Thutmose I and his mother Senseneb and other colorful depictions in Hatshepsut Temple's inner reaches.

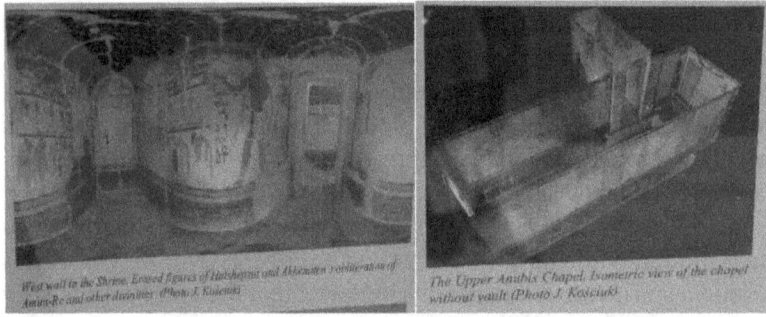

Deir el Bahari 111b. Erased figures of Hatshepsut and Akhenaten's obliteration of Amon-Re and other divinities; and, an isometric view of the Upper Anubis Chapel without vault. (J. Kosciuk's Photos)

Deir el Bahari 112. Close-up of the engaged columns of the Portico entrancing the Sanctuary or "Holy of Holies," viewed from the north.

HATSHEPSUT'S TEMPLE AT DEIR EL BAHARI

Deir el Bahari 113. Close-up of the engaged columns of the Portico entrancing the Sanctuary or "Holy of Holies," viewed from the south.

22. FINE ART. THE EGYPT EXPLORATION FUND. "DEIR EL BAHARI." *The Academy* 49 No. 1254 (May 16, 1896: 412-413).

Malaguey: May 2, 1896.

The student of Egyptian art, and especially of Egyptian architecture, has now at his disposal on the spot every facility for the study of a monument unique among all those preserved to us in the Valley of the Nile. The temple of Deir el Bahari is completely cleared, and is now free from the last of the rubbish mounds which last year still encumbered its enclosure wall on the south.

FREDERICK MONDERSON

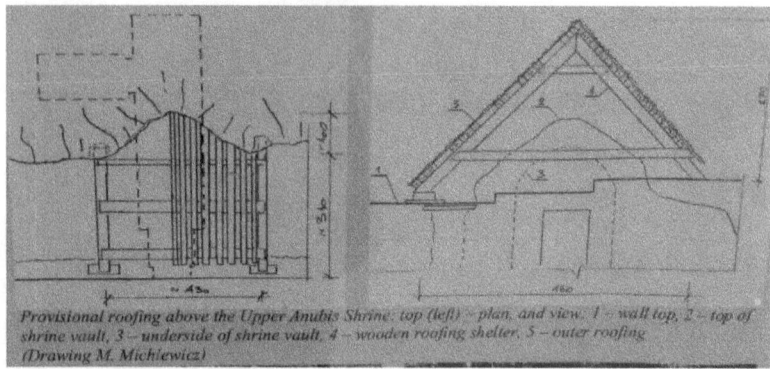

Deir el Bahari 113a. Provisional roofing above the Anubis Shrine (top left); shrine vault; underside of shrine vault; wooden shelter; and outer roofing. (Drawing M. Michiewicz)

Deir el Bahari 114. Symbols of Egyptian health and long life.

Even the casual visitor is immediately struck by the fact that this temple is unlike any other, both in plan and in the details of style adopted in its construction by the architect, Senmut. There is no other Egyptian temple known to us, which is built on a rising

HATSHEPSUT'S TEMPLE AT DEIR EL BAHARI

succession of platforms; and we are therefore without comparison for our guidance in seeking to ascertain how the architect was led to the adoption of this scheme. To some extent it may have been suggested to him by the nature of the site at his disposal, by the huge step in which the rock of the foundation descends to the plain. What was the distinctive use of each of the three platforms on which the temple was built? Our excavations have proved that the lowest platform was treated as the garden or rather the orchard, of the temple, and that the trees planted in it were artificially watered. But the central and most extensive platform, on the one side abutting against the cliffs, and on the other supported by a decorated retaining wall, seems to have been a clear space, and may perhaps be considered as corresponding to the spacious colonnaded courts preceding the sanctuaries in temples of both Pharaohs and the Ptolemies. Neither have we any certainty as to the proposed use of the four unfinished chambers opening to the colonnade on the northern side of the middle platform. Like the lateral chambers at Denderah and Edfu, they may have been intended as storerooms for the incense and sacred oils, the garments and numerous utensils necessary to performing the various rites of the complicated Egyptian ritual. Or, like the court of the altar of Harmachis, they may have been sanctuaries dedicated to the cult of divinities more especially worshipped in other parts of Egypt. But the more plausible supposition is that they were meant to be funerary chapels for members of the queen's family.

Deir el Bahari 114a. The Upper Court's Northern Wall with doorway (right) to Court of Ra-Horakhty's in situ altar of 10 steps.

FREDERICK MONDERSON

Deir el Bahari 115. Another look at the Temple from the mountain and the surrounding terrain, in and beyond the amphitheater.

The above may serve as examples of the many unsolved questions raised by the study of this remarkable building; and the solution of the problems is the more interesting, since Deir el Bahari is the oldest of all the funerary temples in the so-called Memnonia of Thebes.

Again, the similarity of the architecture at Deir el Bahari to that of Greek temples is forced upon us, especially when looking on the white columns of the Anubis Shrine after coming from the Ramesseum. This impression is not only a general one, but is borne out in some detail by a comparison between the fluted columns of Hatshepsut and those of the Doric order, by a consideration of the architectural proportions of this part of the building and the relations between column and architrave. At Deir el Bahari nothing is on a gigantic scale; but it seems to me that when the Egyptians turned aside from the style which was here applied so successfully, in favor of the more massive architecture of Karnak and Medinet Habu, they

HATSHEPSUT'S TEMPLE AT DEIR EL BAHARI

deviated from the path which would have led them to elegance, and preferred the majestic and the colossal.

At the end of last winter, it could indeed be said that the temple was practically cleared. Nevertheless, the excavation was at some point incomplete; and the work of last season, which has been on a much larger scale than that of the preceding, has now completed it. Last year the enclosure wall on the south was still encumbered, and the retaining wall to the Hathor Shrine was visible to but half its depth; now the enclosure wall is not entirely bared, but it is divided by a wide open space from the mounds of rubbish which cover tombs and structures older than the temple of Hatshepsu.

In the course of this year's work, we have found many fragments of the famous Punt sculptures, all emphasizing the African character of the country in which the expedition landed, but testifying also the fact that the population of that country was not homogeneous. In addition to the genuine Puntites, with aquiline features, pointed beards, and long hair, there are also represented Negroes of two different shades of color – brown and black. The native huts were apparently made of wickerwork, and in front of one of them sits a big white dog with pendant ears. Another dog of the same kind, and led by a string, is being brought to the Egyptians. Birds with long bills are seen flying out of the trees from which men are gathering the incense, while the nests which they have forsaken are robbed of their eggs either for food or for some religious observance. Unfortunately, these precious fragments do not complete the missing scenes, of which the destruction must not be attributed wholly to tourists and antiquity dealers: this work of havoc was begun in ancient times.

FREDERICK MONDERSON

Deir el Bahari 116. Close-up of the Second Ramp, Middle and Upper Colonnades and the Upper Court with its Peristyle of two rows of columns before the Hypostyle Hall. Beyond is a better view of Mentuhotep's Temple.

The Hathor Shrine projects beyond the southern edge of the middle platform. Parallel to the Shrine a wall branched off at right angles to the enclosure wall forming a small court already destroyed in the time of the XXIst Dynasty. The corner of the wall alone remains. Our excavations in the soil of this court and along the outside of the shrine confirm Mariette's discovery that the temple was built on the site of a necropolis of the XIth Dynasty. In the immediate vicinity of the temple, I came across some dozen tombs, which I thoroughly cleared, finding that, as usual in most Egyptian cemeteries, they had all been anciently rifled. Some had been reused in the XXIst Dynasty for priests of Amon. But even in a rifled necropolis we may hope to discover occasionally a tomb, which was overlooked by the plunderers, and to this end it is necessary that every tomb in the place should be systematically excavated. The tombs at Deir el Bahari are all on the same plan; they are rectangular pits dug in the soft and flaky rock to a depth of ten or twelve feet. On one side, generally on the west, opens a small chamber originally close by a brick wall, which contained one coffin only. The plundering of

HATSHEPSUT'S TEMPLE AT DEIR EL BAHARI

those tombs had usually taken place shortly after burial; and in such cases the rubbish with which they were filled consisted of the rock chips made in the course of cutting out the pit. Several pits, which, judging from the nature of the rubbish they contained, apparently untouched, proved to have been completely cleared except for a few wooden figures, or a little coarse pottery. But when a pit contained stones, some of which had obviously been taken from the walls of the temple, there could be no doubt that the tomb had been re-used; and in one case the door had been closed with two or three stone slabs, and the tomb itself contained a yellow mummiform coffin of XXIst Dynasty style.

Deir el Bahari 117. Close-up of the Second Ramp, Middle and Upper Colonnades, Upper Terrace with its Osiride Statues and Upper Court with its Peristyle Colonnade.

The interments of the XIth Dynasty were apparently made with a certain amount of luxury, and the tombs originally contained valuables, otherwise they would not have tempted the cupidity of the robbers. I would form some idea as to the character of this necropolis must once have been from a tomb which had been only

FREDERICK MONDERSON

partly plundered. In emptying the pit, we found two pieces of the gilt case of the inner coffin, and the blue glazed-ware bead necklace of the mummy. The chamber contained a coffin in the style of the XIth Dynasty, made of sycamore wood, rectangular, very thick and heavy, and in a perfect state of preservation. Outside, on box and lid, are lines of blue hieroglyphs giving the names of the deceased, and also there are two large eyes, a decoration characteristic of the coffins of that period. The angles are lined with gilding. The inside is entirely covered with paintings and inscriptions. Above are horizontal lines of large hieroglyphs most exquisitely painted, as well as representations of the objects supposed to be placed near the deceased: mirrors, necklaces, bracelets, etc. Below and on the bottom are funerary texts, in a script intermediate between hieratic and hieroglyphic. In the coffin had been left pieces of a very thick cartonnage, entirely gilt, except the necklace, which was painted in colors, and the hair. The mummy must have had jewels, which had been stolen, but the plundering seems to have been done hastily. The sandals and the pillow, both gilt, had been left, as well as many objects, which had been deposited near the coffin. These objects are similar to those discovered at Meir in tombs of the VIth Dynasty, but they are of less artistic value. We got out two wooden boats with their crews, in one of which the figure of the deceased is seen sitting under an awning; two models of houses containing numerous figures – one of them emptying bags of corn into a granary; in the other a bull is seen lying on the ground, with his legs tied together while a man cuts his throat with a knife. We also found statuettes of men and women, carrying jars, loaves, and various provisions in baskets. These objects recall some adjuncts of the earthly life of the deceased, and were intended to answer the same purpose as the pictures on the walls of the tombs at Ghizeh and Sakkara. There is hardly a single tomb in which some such model figures had not been dropped. In one they had been jumbled together into a corner with the bricks of the door, in order to make room for the mummy of a priest of Amon, evidently of no high rank, since it was his office to prepare ointments for the use of the high priest.

HATSHEPSUT'S TEMPLE AT DEIR EL BAHARI

Deir el Bahari 118. The line down the center of the second Ramp is clearly visible in this photo of the upper reaches of the Temple.

It is remarkable that this beautiful coffin does not bear the same name inside and out. Inside the deceased is called *Buan*. He was a man of high rank with numerous titles, among which are those of Head of the Treasury and Head of the Granaries, showing that his position was one of considerable power. But on the outside, he is called simply *Mentuhotep*, a name probably assumed as being that of the king under whose reign he had spent the greater part of his life, or to whom he was most indebted for the favors which he had received. I take it that the life of *Buan-Mentuhotep* was contemporary with the end of the XIth Dynasty and the beginning of the XIIth. His coffin, with all its paraphernalia, is now at Ghizeh. In artistic beauty and in preservation it is certainly one of the finest to be found in any museum.

As my work was exclusively directed towards the temple and all that concerned its structure and history, I did not go out of my way to make further researches in the XIth Dynasty necropolis. It is a place where interesting and probably fruitful excavations might be made; and I believe that a systematic exploration of the space between the temple and the cliffs which bounds the amphitheater of Deir el Bahari on the south would reveal not only the whole extent of the necropolis, of which we have investigated one outskirt only, but also remains of buildings erected by Antefs and Mentuhoteps, kings whose dates and succession are now the object of much discussion among Egyptologists. EDOUARD NAVILLE.

Deir el Bahari 119. Still closer view of the Upper Colonnade and the visitors.

23. Deir el Bahari: A Final Reflection or Postscript
By
Frederick Monderson

Hatshepsut's temple at Deir el Bahari is undoubtedly one of the most beautiful, if not the most beautiful and admired of sites on the tourist circuit in today's Egypt, North East Africa. Interestingly, if transported back into ancient times to view this structure in all its glory, one would be many times more astonished by its beauty and functional features that reflect the magnificent edifice the author and

HATSHEPSUT'S TEMPLE AT DEIR EL BAHARI

originators imagined when they planned, executed, constructed, completed and put into service this religious and mortuary edifice to please their God and Queen.

The temple in its glorious days excited and sparked the imagination of the ancients as it delights the cognitive conception of moderns who incidentally have the benefit of the history of architectural accomplishments with which to compare. Keep in mind that original constructions leave modern imitations struggling in the dust of previous creations that have already established yardsticks by which to measure subsequent structures. That is, original building had no edifices to copy! In a twist, however, Hatshepsut's temple copied Mentuhotep's 11th Dynasty temple, with some added features. We do not have any evidence, on the other hand, of what influenced Mentuhotep's temple.

Deir el Bahari 120. The Upper Terrace has 1 statue for each of the 22 pillars and four abutting the entrance for a total of 26 statues in the glory days of the Temple.

FREDERICK MONDERSON

Even more, nevertheless, the temple of Hatshepsut at Deir el Bahari, while an imitation of the earlier 11th Dynasty temple of Mentuhotep, five hundred years in existence previously, still has to be considered an original imitation! Its durability has allowed it to withstand the ravages of time and ancient and modern man and in its preserved state stands as a testimony to early African creativity along the banks of the Nile River. Interesting, when Hatshepsut's temple was built, the temple of Mentuhotep, built five hundred years previously and then in existence forced the former to occupy limited space in the amphitheater that houses these buildings. And, now 3500 years later Hatshepsut's structure is still standing, the Step Pyramid, the Pyramids of Ghizeh, temples and tombs of the New Kingdom and later, makes it crystal clear these early African builders erected their structures for eternity and accomplished the immortality they set out to achieve. What other constructions on which continent can make similar boasts? At best ancient creations outside of Africa can only boast of being enshrined in myth or viewed as archaic ruins fueled by the myths behind their creations and the propaganda that propel those myths.

As such, when one considers the nature, pronouncements and notions on evidence of the wonders of the ancient world, and the assaults they have been exposed to and been victims of, compared with Hatshepsut's temple and how it has withstood those assaults, one has to echo Dr. Yosef ben-Jochannan's sentiments, 'Why has the Temple of Hatshepsut at Deir el Bahari not been considered a wonder of the ancient world?' Equally, when we consider the ancient Greeks designation of the eight wonders of the world, only the pyramids of Egypt have withstood the ravages of time, have remained standing and are far from being a memory or myth. Three and a half thousand years later, the Temple at Deir el Bahari rivals the pyramids in the number of visitors, the distance they travel to view it and the appreciation of its aesthetic beauty that the modern conception can more greatly admire and appreciate.

HATSHEPSUT'S TEMPLE AT DEIR EL BAHARI

Deir el Bahari 121. Close-up of the visitors in the Upper Court and before the Portico fronting the entrance to the "Holy of Holies."

Recently, a modern movement debated, created conventions and chose a new collection of marvels designated wonders of the world. Not discounting the beauty and wonderful nature of these new marvels, many natural not man-made, Hatshepsut's Temple at Deir el Bahari was cheated a second time. Having been a marvel in ancient times and still retains that beauty and mystique over a span of several millennia of years, perhaps a new category of marvels needs be created with this wonderful ancient creation that still inspires the most breathtaking admiration for artistic beauty, architectural permanence, admirable aesthetics and prolific detail.

There is no question Deir el Bahari is a remarkable structure, unusual in its plan and equally unusual in its details. Granted today we know the temple was patterned after Mentuhotep's earlier building, but it is more beautiful than its prototype. The queen's temple was called *Zosret* and the "Holy of Holies" *Zoser-Zosru*. Side by side with the earlier structure it was called *Zosreti*, the "Two Holies." Nevertheless, there were many innovative features Senmut added that not only sets his structure apart but revolutionized and gives evidence of his thinking as architect and administrator. This is made more real as he utilized the equally unusual terrain opting not to use height but lines and open space filled with detail.

Deir el Bahari 122. The two Ramps and the Colonnades in this view from the mountain.

Senmut began by using nature themes as birds, water plants, garden themes, flowers, fishes, and Persea and papyrus trees. In the decoration he added a multitude of other features including soldiers, archers, trumpeters, standards, lions, panthers, etc. He built his tomb within the temple precinct. There was a Valley Temple and a sphinx and tree- lined causeway from the waterside to the Pylon entrance. He included depictions of river transport of obelisks on barges and the most remarkable anthropological details of the Punt expedition, as well as the birth phenomenon of the queen. This particular theory of divine origin was original and really revolutionary. It was eventually copied by Amenhotep III at Luxor Temple and much later by Alexander the great.

The chapels of the Hathor and Anubis divinities and the location at the northern and southern extremities of the temples, neatly tucked

HATSHEPSUT'S TEMPLE AT DEIR EL BAHARI

away, are a hallmark of Egyptian thinking. Columns and pillars decorating these shrines are worthy of note. The creative genius Senmut also featured numerous gods enumerated in the birth phenomenon, the dedication and events of the ritual and worship. Employing courts, ramps, three platforms, terraces, colonnades and arrangement of colonnades was significant. Lions looking out added security and divinity watch features. Incense trees were planted before the pylon and there were plants in the gardens. He featured "milk ponds" to assuage the divinities' thirst and taste. Alternating columns with pillars as well as use of round and proto-Doric columns was also revolutionary. He included many Osiride and other statues of the queen and other gods including himself. As architect, he constructed a tomb within the precinct for his final repose, an unthinkable act, but with the most unusual astronomical and heavenly charts. Utilizing the mountain as a backdrop was a challenge and the color reflected from the mountain was also significant as an aesthetic appetizer. He used niches on the upper platform court with Osiride statues of the Queen.

Deir el Bahari 123. Uraeus and the Pharaonic eagle wearing the Double Crown and sun disk with uraeus and ankh.

FREDERICK MONDERSON

Deir el Bahari 124. Mut, wearing vulture headdress and with scepter and ankh (left) faces Osiris (right) with crook and flail, instruments of his power.

There was a portico to the main sanctuary and an open-air altar with stairs as well as altars in the chapels. Senmut included chambers and chapels for storage of garments, utensils and unguents as well as literature of the daily temple ritual. Several sanctuaries are included in the structure. Various walls, viz., enclosure, retaining, building, etc., adds to the repertoire and were beautifully decorated. The bas-relief has retained its decoration with fine color remarkably well. The architect secretly inserted an untold number of statues of himself in different parts of the temple that were not all found and destroyed by his adversaries. He included tools and personal artifacts of the owner as part of the foundation ritual that was customary at every temple's beginning. To coin a phrase, "pound for pound" this temple is incomparable with any other in Egypt. Its art matches any structure dating throughout Egyptian history. When all the chips are counted, it has survived history and stands as majestic as when it was first constructed and put into service. Perhaps a ventured thought is that only the love of a woman could

HATSHEPSUT'S TEMPLE AT DEIR EL BAHARI

motivate a man to produce such an unsurpassed and beautiful work with architectural, artistic and aesthetic appeal.

Baikie (1932: 415-16) in commentary on the structure as the Queen's mortuary temple, underscores the genius behind the planning of a tunnel to her tomb. He tells us, its "original idea seems to have been that the sarcophagus-chamber of her tomb in the Valley of the Kings should lie immediately beneath the great temple, whose axis was arranged to be in line with that of the tomb beyond the cliffs at el-Deir el-Bahari. Unfortunately, however, the rock in the place which the Queen had chosen for her resting-place turned out to be bad, so that it was not possible to carry out the intention of burrowing beneath the cliffs till a position beneath the temple was reached; and the 700-foot corridor of the tomb had to be turned in a great curve away from its projected objective."

Senmut also substituted majestic elegance for the massive and colossal. There were later tomb burials and the temple was later re-used for religious purposes by members of other faiths. Even much later it became a sanatorium with healing attributes. It's amazing that the temple has retained so much of its beauty into modern times being victimized several times over. It was first victimized by the wrath of Thutmose and his adherents, the zealots of Akhnaton's Amarna heresy, inferior repairs were done by Rameses II, Coptic monks rearranged much of the art and architecture to suit their purposes, Christian zealots were never kind to it, and native Islamic and foreign treasure hunters, time, weather and climate have all left impressions on it. Nevertheless, like Maya Angelou's poem, the spirits of the temple may today boast, "Still I rise" to show my beauty.

Baikie offers two quotations that not simply reflect the beauty of Deir el Bahari but also underscore some of the malicious damage done to this wonderful work of art. The first quote refers to evidence found in the Chapel of Anubis, on the northern half of the Middle Colonnade where Baikie mentions erasures and two scenes. Here, Baikie (1932: 41) describes the first scene on the western wall of

FREDERICK MONDERSON

the doorway into Anubis' Chapel. "In the one to the south (left-hand) of the door, Amen-Re is enthroned before an immense mass of offerings which the queen is presenting to him. Hatshepsut's figure is erased, as usual; but Amun has in this case escaped the fanaticism of Akhenaten's agents. The especially noteworthy detail of the scene, however, is the vulture of El-Kab which hovers above the head of the erased figure of Hatshepsut. Its color is remarkably well preserved, and both as a design and as a piece of coloring the figure is very fine. The scene to the north of the doorway represents Hatshepsut (again erased) offering a similar mass of gifts before Anubis. The hawk of Edfu, which hovers above Hatshepsut, is another example of fine design and color, though its color scheme is lower than that of the vulture."

"The north wall has a small recess, on the right hand of which are figures of various divinities. Above the recess is a figure of Thutmose III offering wine to Sokar, a god of the dead. On the left hand of the recess another decorative vulture hovers above another erased figure of Hatshepsut. The south wall has an erased figure of Hatshepsut between Harmachis and Nekhbet, and again a finely colored hawk, displayed, hovers above the queen. The end of the inner chamber of the shrine has a fine scene of Hatshepsut (erased) between Anubis and Hathor, with above the usual couchant jackals, and over all the winged sun-disk."

The blight of erasure is even more evident on the Birth Colonnade, even more so, because the Queen's people innovated an idea that was hard to question and certainly had much favor in its connection with the great New Empire god Amun. Baikie (1932: 418) discusses: "The reliefs on the rear wall of which represent the state fiction by which Hatshepsut was regarded as the actual child of Amun by the Queen Ahmose, the wife of Tuthmosis I." Accordingly, in this respect Baikie (1932: 418-419) wrote: "The series has suffered considerably both from family jealousies and religious prejudices; and Rameses II has not improved things by the crude coloring with which he has bedaubed the delicate reliefs. The scenes begin at the south end of the colonnade, next the ascending ramp, with a council of the gods in the presence of Amun. Then we

HATSHEPSUT'S TEMPLE AT DEIR EL BAHARI

see Thoth leading Amun (both entirely erased) into the chamber of Queen Ahmose, and next Amun seated face to face with the queen, and impregnating her with the ankh, the divine breath of life, which is held to her nose. The seats on which the god and the queen are seated are borne up in the heavens, as in the parallel scene of Amenophis III at Luxor, by two goddesses who sit upon a lion-headed couch. Then we see the ram-headed creator-god Khnum, getting instructions from Amun, and (partly erased) shaping Hatshepsut and her Ka upon his potter's wheel, while the frog-headed goddess Heqt puts the breath of life into the nostrils of the newly created babe. Thoth appears to Queen Ahmose, and warns her of her approaching accouchement; and Khnum and Heqt lead the queen to the birth-chamber."

Deir el Bahari 125. Sokar, ancient Theban god of the dead (left) and enthroned Amon (right) are two deities in this temple.

FREDERICK MONDERSON

Baikie (1932: 419) says further in an assessment but even more important he highlights the sin against art and the temple. "The scene of the birth is very remarkable, and is handled with great reticence and delicacy. The queen sits on a chair with her women attending on her. The chair is placed on a lion-headed couch, which is upheld by various gods, and stands in turn on another lion-headed couch, also supported beneath by gods. Among the deities in the scene are Bes and Thoueris (Taurt), the hideous patrons of child-birth. Hathor next presents Hatshepsut to Amun, and twelve goddesses suckle the twelve Kas of the divine child. Next Thoth and Amun hold the child and her Ka (erased in both cases). Finally, Hatshepsut and her Ka (both erased) are seen in the hand of various goddesses, and Safkhet, the recording goddess of history, writes the record of her birth. The remaining scenes of the north colonnade refer to the queen's presentation to the gods of Egypt, her presentation by her earthly father, Thutmosis I, to the magnates of the land, and her coronation."

Deir el Bahari 126. Dominion, stability and life are universal pharaonic symbols found in this temple.

HATSHEPSUT'S TEMPLE AT DEIR EL BAHARI

Deir el Bahari 127. Lapwings and boat's ram-head symbol.

Deir el Bahari 128. Hatshepsut in Karnak. The "Red Chapel" of Queen Hatshepsut reconstructed and now in the "Open Air Museum" that was once considered Karnak Temple's Sanctuary.

FREDERICK MONDERSON

Deir el Bahari 129. Hatshepsut in Karnak. A side view of the "Red Chapel" considered the Sanctuary at Karnak under Hatshepsut that was demolished by Thutmose III's hordes and now reconstructed in the Open Air Museum.

Deir el Bahari 130. Hatshepsut in Karnak. One of the few images of Hatshepsut in the "Red Chapel" that escaped the despoilers hands showing the Queen pouring a Libation onto Min, the ithyphallic form of Amun.

HATSHEPSUT'S TEMPLE AT DEIR EL BAHARI

The underlying reality presented here are the replete erasures and the psychology behind the damages done here at the colonnade, in the chapels, in the Upper Court, and elsewhere. In fact, wherever Thutmose's people could find evidence of the queen they did their dirty work. The same can be said for Akhenaton's people but with a different intent. Nevertheless, and despite all of the animosity expressed here the temple was still able to retain its majesty, dignity and artistic beauty, perhaps because the architect had a premonition or foresaw the assault on his work of art as he did on his tomb. As such then, he built to withstand all forms of calamity and this is shown with the passage of time as his work retains much of its original aura.

Deir el Bahari 131. Hatshepsut in Karnak. The Queen's fallen obelisk (near) and her standing (right) obelisk beside her father Thutmose I's (left) with the ruins of the Hypostyle Hall to the further left.

These then are some of the features that make Deir el Bahari such a remarkable structure with its unusual details attesting to Senmut's brilliance as architect as well as administrator. Hence, one can easily affirm: "Architecturally, Hatasu's Temple has no parallel: in the quality and preservation of its painted reliefs, it vies with any of the best known tombs; it is placed in a grander situation than any other building in Egypt."

FREDERICK MONDERSON

Deir el Bahari 132. Hatshepsut in Karnak. The "Red Chapel." Hatshepsut kneels to present two vessels to the enthroned Theban Triad with evidence of the Queen's Cartouche or Shennu nearby.

Deir el Bahari 133. Hatshepsut in Karnak. The "Red Chapel." Wearing the Red Crown and holding a whisk, Hatshepsut dances before the Ark of Amun, at rest.

If the visitor can effectively savor a fraction of this list the trip is worth the journey and cost. Equally, as Flinders Petrie has pointed-out, the kaleidoscope view of the play of light on the color scheme of the mountain as a background as the sun sets in the late afternoon, makes this amazing site one that retains its timeless mystique and metaphysical and spiritual effluence. Deir el Bahari is truly a godly structure with a timelessness that speaks volumes of ancient African man's adoration of his gods and his women.

HATSHEPSUT'S TEMPLE AT DEIR EL BAHARI

Deir el Bahari 134. A much better view of Mentuhotep's Temple from the mountain's "Bird's Eye View."

24. NEW REVELATIONS ABOUT EGYPT'S QUEEN HATSHEPSUT
By
Dr. Fred Monderson

Today especially, many women want to be considered same as "The First Queen," who incidentally has been resurrected from oblivion thanks to historical sleuthing through the use of archaeological, forensic, dental and scientific evidence techniques. Recently, Dr. Zahi Hawass, Secretary General of the Supreme Antiquities Council called for a radical re-evaluation of the identities of all ancient Egyptian mummies for, despite what is known of Who's Who; none of the names of Egypt's kings, queens and nobles are unquestionably certain. That is, with the exception of King

FREDERICK MONDERSON

Tutankhamon who was found entombed in his burial chamber as he was laid to rest more than three thousand years ago. Such is the price of certainty! Now, however, the mummy of Queen Hatshepsut has been positively identified and has joined this illustrious and solo historical figure in revealing her unquestioned identity thanks to modern scientific methods of investigation.

Queen Hatshepsut, Ma'at-Ka-Ra, came to power in the 16th Century B.C. as the fourth/fifth ruler of the 18th Dynasty, New Kingdom, and ruled for nearly twenty years. Daring to challenge male domination of kingly rule in the ancient world, Hatshepsut ruled well, was well-liked by her people, accomplished a great deal and engendered enmity by many who, in turn, contributed greatly to her demise and unleashed great retribution to her name, memory and monuments. Even in death, the Queen's resting place was attacked, fire-bombed and her mummy equally received the same treatment. Such efforts by individuals who developed a hatred for the queen intended that her name and memory be erased from history and were, to some extent, successful in their nefarious deeds. However, fate intervened and despite malice, the well-preserved mummy was discovered in 1903 in an obscure tomb, number 60, in the Valley of the Kings. At the end of the recent scientific investigation, in a telephone conversation quoted in *The New York Times* of June 27, 2007, p. A 6, 4, Mr. Hawass boldly asserted "We have scientific proof that this is the mummy of Queen Hatshepsut." In addition, the article, stated: "DNA analysis revealed a family relationship between the obese woman and Queen Aahmose-Nefertari, matriarch of the 18th dynasty."

An old adage, "What happens in the dark will eventually come to light" applies admirably to the case and treatment of Queen Hatshepsut as she has been rescued from the oblivion to which her enemies consigned her. Regarding these adversaries of the Queen, whose dark deeds were done in light of ancient times and circumstances, historical scrutiny has revealed a remarkable woman whose efforts have impacted art, architecture, religious practice and even archaeology and remains endeared in the minds and hearts of

HATSHEPSUT'S TEMPLE AT DEIR EL BAHARI

modern lovers of antiquarian studies. Adding to this latter, scientific sleuthing has been able to correctly identify the queen, whose mummy has lain in oblivion for more than a century after its discovery and thanks to these efforts the Queen joined the young king and their identities are now unmistakably certain.

Despite early absence from the historical record, what we know of Queen Hatshepsut is that she succeeded to becoming Pharaoh through a number of strategies including aligning with strong males in her kingdom, courting the powerful religious body of the Amon priesthood, building extensive civic and religious structures and initiating many pharaonic features that would remain essential Egyptian practices. Undertaking far-flung expeditions of an economic and anthropological and historic nature, and concocting significant stratagems that reinforced the view pharaoh was considered a divine person, Hatshepsut certainly impacted Egyptian history. The people of her realm respected and loved Hatshepsut even though she was a woman who ruled as pharaoh and they did not think this state of affairs would bring ill-fortune to the nation. Yet, recognizing her limitations as a female, she ruled as a man or king; dressed as a male; wore a false beard; and considering that pharaoh was the "Son of God Ra," while having a tomb in the Valley of the Queens, she proclaimed herself "Son of Ra" and had another tomb dug in the Valley of the Kings.

It's been argued, one of the reasons she was disliked after death is because she built her mortuary temple at Deir el Bahari bigger than that of her ancestor Mentuhotep II whose nearby Middle Kingdom temple in the amphitheater was in fact transitional from the Old to New Kingdom architectural style and also her prototype. This remarkable woman even planned a tunnel linking her temple with her tomb in the Valley of the Kings so that upon her death and the attendant ceremony she would be transported directly to the tomb through this passageway. Unfortunately, the ground between the two mortuary structures beneath the surrounding mountains was too soft to sustain the tunnel and the idea was abandoned.

FREDERICK MONDERSON

Nevertheless, the temple at Deir el Bahari came to reflect the crowning glory of the Queen's accomplishments, because it blended artistic and architectural splendor as well as philosophical creativity to justify an act of divine intervention in kingly conception. It recounted an important pioneering anthropological and economic undertaking that also facilitated the trans-shipment of rare animals and transplanting of trees, an incense plant, to decorate the holy place and to assuage the spiritual and esoteric appetite of the deity who commanded such an undertaking. The removal and transshipment of botanical specimens that were replanted at the temple was a revolutionary botanical feat that proved plants could thrive in distances far removed from their original habitat.

A long standing challenge to archaeologists and Egyptologists has been the desire to identify the names of significant individuals of ancient Egypt whose remains have been recovered. This has particularly been so since the discovery of the "Deir el Bahari cache" of distinguished New Kingdom personalities in 1881. This was enhanced by the second discovery of mummies in the tomb of Amenhotep II in the late 1890s. In the renowned 1881 discovery, while "big name" kings and queens were identified, the name of Ma'at-Ka-Ra stirred sensation in many that the mummy of Queen Hatshepsut was recovered. As it turned out, the Ma'at Ka Ra whose mummy was recovered was in fact a 22nd Dynasty Queen. Apparently, the custom of taking the name of an illustrious ancestor found great fruition particularly in the 19th and 20th Dynasties among the Ramesside kings. Thus, despite the efforts to erase Hatshepsut's name by her adversaries, the 22nd Dynasty Queen found great favor in adopting the name Ma'at Ka Ra. As this mix-up was soon discovered, the intrigue and question as to the true identity of Hatshepsut continued well past the discovery of two mummies in an obscure tomb in 1903.

In *Egypt and its Monuments*: *Pharaoh, Fellahs and Explorers* (New York: Harper and Brothers, 1891: 268) Amelia B. Edwards paid a wonderful tribute to Hatshepsut with the following statement: "Throughout the years of Hatasu's sole reign the land of Egypt appears to have enjoyed an interval of profound peace, during which

HATSHEPSUT'S TEMPLE AT DEIR EL BAHARI

she taxed the resources of her empire by repairing those shrines and temples which had gone to ruin during the period of Hyksos rule; by embellishing and enriching Karnak; and by erecting a sumptuous temple in Western Thebes. In those works, she proved herself to be one of the most magnificent builder-sovereigns of Egypt. Of the victories of Thothmes III, there remain only the long lists of conquered nations and captive cities which he caused to be sculptured on the pylons of Karnak; but the Temple of Dayr-el-Bahari and the two great obelisks of Karnak, much as they have suffered at the hands of Time the Destroyer, are to this day permanent records of the tranquil reign of Hatasu."

"Amen Khnum Hatasu, the Golden Horus, Lord of the two Lands, hath dedicated to her father Amen of Thebes, two obelisks of Mahet stone [red granite], hewn from the quarries of the South. Their summits [pyramidions] were sheated with pure gold, taken from the chiefs of all nations."

"His majesty gave these two gilded obelisks to her father Amen that her name should live forever in this temple."

"Each is one single shaft of red Mahet stone, without joint or rivet. They are seen from both banks of the Nile, and when Ra arises betwixt them as he journeys upward from the heavenly horizon, they flood the two Egypt's with the glory of their brightness."

"His Majesty began this work in the fifteenth year of her reign, the first day of the month of Mehir, and finished it on the last day of the month of Mesore, in her sixteenth year."

Edwards (1891: 269) goes on to point out how the Queen and the young prince were represented on the obelisk, in the following statement: "The shaft of this obelisk bears on its western and southern sides long dedicatory inscriptions in the name of Hatasu only; whereas on the eastern side we find, to the right and left of the central column of hieroglyphs, two outer columns in which Hatasu and Thothmes III are represented together in adoration before various manifestations of Amen-Ra. The fact that the name of Thothmes III here appears with that of his sister in the sixteenth year of her reign acquires an especial interest when it is remembered that this is the same date at which we meet with it before .... It seems, therefore, to mark the precise time at which he was finally recognized." Finally, Edwards mentions how though Thutmose's backlash erased the Queen's name from her monuments and inserted either that of Thutmose II or himself, these names themselves employ "masculine titles with feminine pronouns."

Notwithstanding, anyone familiar with modern efforts to enhance, preserve and safeguard the monuments of Egypt must give great praise to the Supreme Antiquities Council under the efforts of the tireless Zahi Hawass. From what has been said about Zahi Hawass, his enthusiasm is exacerbated when a challenge such as posed by Hatshepsut's identity presents itself and with some encouragement, the project was successful. Of course, success breeds success and without a doubt utilizing the same methodology and strategies, many more similar mummies will, hopefully, be identified. Meanwhile, Hatshepsut's accomplishments continue to intrigue, motivate and astonish visitors to the temple who still marvel at her most imposing wonders, Deir el Bahari and the obelisks at Karnak that stand as testimony of what a woman's love for god, her family, people and nation can create despite what challenges, man and time, can present.

HATSHEPSUT'S TEMPLE AT DEIR EL BAHARI

Deir el Bahari 135. Image of a Nile god presenting vessels to the Temple (left); and decoration in the temple.

25. CONCLUSIONS

The Temple of Deir el Bahari constructed for Queen Hatshepsut by her architect Senmut, is indeed an enduring construction, that showcased the wonderful art and architectural accomplishments of the early Eighteenth Dynasty. The superabundance of detail this early in history sets the work apart. Importantly, the queen's legacy is intertwined with the leading men who surrounded her and carried out her wishes, helped her rule and maintain power in a male dominated world filled with treachery. Many of them suffered for their close association with this woman pharaoh. Not all did feel the wrath of Tuthmosid avenging associates, but those who did were severely punished, their names expunged and their final resting places wrecked and desecrated. Despite this form of retribution their names have survived to be admired as men who stood by a strong woman and a noble and principled cause and left their impressions, for all to see, on the times in which they lived.

FREDERICK MONDERSON

Deir el Bahari 136. View of the southern wall from the east beside the temple of Mentuhotep's own grounds.

Having said that, the temple itself, which also suffered at the hands of the despoilers, is in some ways a biography of the Queen, is not as Medinet Habu is the principal record of the reign of Rameses III, but Deir el Bahari recounts the significant epochs in the life of Hatshepsut, as it memorialized a daring and avant-garde African Queen represented in an architectural marvel. It tells of her virgin birth; two obelisks she erected at Karnak and the work that went into their erection; the Punt Expedition is a creative anthropological study providing examples of the flora and fauna of that age and region, as well as the bringing of incense trees, over long distances, and replanting them in the temple is significant as migration of botanical species. It was smart thinking to dedicate the temple to several gods, Amon-Ra, Hathor, Anubis, Ra-Horakhty, as well as

HATSHEPSUT'S TEMPLE AT DEIR EL BAHARI

herself, and Tuthmose I and III. This may have blunted the axe of the destroyers; who, none-the-less, got their pound of flesh! The artist Senmut's choice of the location, setting and employment of lines, depth, courts, colonnades, ramps and terraces with the mountain and its splendid color kaleidoscope rather than massiveness was brilliant, in fact genius, on the part of the decision makers.

Deir el Bahari 137. One of surviving images of Queen Hatshepsut showing her straight beard, while gods generally have curved beards.

FREDERICK MONDERSON

The art is enduring. Its association with the notion of Hathor coming out of the mountains, the role of Anubis, god of the dead in this sacred place, and its proximity to the place where the dead enter the underworld, has made Deir el Bahari the wonder that it is. The notion of a tunnel from her mortuary temple to her tomb required tunneling through the mountain and its very conception borders on genius. In an age when buildings were of one-story this three-story structure was ahead of its time. That anyone could destroy such a brilliant work of art attests to the hatred Thutmose III's people manifested for the owner and the work's symbolism. Equally, too, despite the work of the wrecking crew, the Amarna vengeance against anything that was associated with Amon-Ra, the ravages of time and modern man's greed and equally destructive nature, all this says lots about the planning, construction and execution of the project we come to know as Deir el Bahari, a temple unlike any in Egypt. From afar this temple stands out with its white limestone against the Theban hills, observed from the bird's eye view of the mountains above it's a work to behold, and as one enters the individual parts in the ascent or descent from the mountain, its beauty captivates and conveys the brilliance of the queen and her architectural companions who put so much into this project. The historical significance and aura of the Deir el Bahari "cache" discovery lends further fame to the temple basking in mythology, mysticism and divine presence. Thus, Deir el Bahari remains a testimony to ingenuity, tenacity, fortitude and cosmological consciousness of an ancient African Queen and the loyal men who helped her seize and maintain power for two decades. Clearly, Hatshepsut deserves rightly to be called "the first queen" for she sailed the Egyptian ship of state as a formidable captain and left a monumental art and architectural contribution to the history of regal construction in the form of her mortuary temple. Today this structure glorifies her country, her reign and her name, despite the trials and tribulations she faced. In Deir el Bahari she is immortalized not simply as builder but also as innovator, administrator and cosmological and philosophical genius.

HATSHEPSUT'S TEMPLE AT DEIR EL BAHARI

Deir el Bahari 138. Defaced illustration kneeling on Heb.

FREDERICK MONDERSON

Deir el Bahari 139. Hatshepsut in Karnak. The "Red Chapel."
A stone container with hollowed-out insides bearing the names of
Thutmose *Men-Khepper-Ra* (left) and Hatshepsut *Ma'at-Ka-Ra*
(right) on the front face.

26. Additional Bibliography

Breasted, J.H. *Ancient Records of Egypt.*
Breasted, J.H. *A History of Egypt.*
Clarke and Engelbach. *Ancient Egyptian Masonry.*
Edgerton. *The Thutmosid Succession* (Studies in Ancient Oriental Civilization 8 (1933: 11-160).
Forman and Vilikmova. *Egyptian Art.*
Gardiner, A. *Egypt of the Pharaohs.*
Giedion. *The Eternal Present.*
Groenewegen-Frankfort. *Arrest and Movement.*
Murray, Margaret. *Egyptian Temples.*
Naville, Edouard. *The Temple of Deir el Bahari.*
Ranke. *The Art of Ancient Egypt.*
Smith, Baldwin. *Egyptian Architecture.*
Smith, S. *Interconnection in the Ancient East.*
Steindorff and Seele. *When Egypt Ruled the East.*

HATSHEPSUT'S TEMPLE AT DEIR EL BAHARI

Stuart. *The Funeral Tent of an Egyptian Queen.* 23-4
Wilkinson, Garner. *The Topography of Thebes.*

Deir el Bahari 140. Hatshepsut in Karnak. The "Red Chapel." Hatshepsut, *Ma'at-Ka-Ra* (left) offers flowers and a plant to the Ark of Amun, while Thutmose III *Men-Khepper-Ra* (right) stands to her rear and offers two vessels.

Deir el Bahari 141. Hatshepsut in Karnak. The "Red Chapel." The Ark of Amun at rest with Hatshepsut's image to the right, defaced as part of the attack against her image and monuments. Notice the necklace to the right of the Ark's bow!

Deir el Bahari 142. Hatshepsut in Karnak. The "Red Chapel." Hatshepsut has prepared a feast for the Theban Triad, the first of whom sits in this frame. However, the Queen's image has been erased to the right before the offerings.

Deir el Bahari 143. Hatshepsut in Karnak. The "Red Chapel." Hatshepsut embraces the god, Amun as Min, who stands firm!

HATSHEPSUT'S TEMPLE AT DEIR EL BAHARI

Deir el Bahari 144. Hatshepsut in Karnak. Seated red granite statue of the Queen near the Sanctuary.

Deir el Bahari 145. Hatshepsut in Karnak. The "Red Chapel." Hatshepsut, *Ma'at-Ka-Ra*, raises her hands in adoration, while Thutmose III, *Men-Khepper-Ra*, stands behind her and prepares to incense the figure of adoration. Notice, she wears a beard and he does not!

Deir el Bahari 146. A final look at the Portico entrance to the Sanctuary in the Upper Court on the Upper Terrace of Hatshepsut's temple.

HATSHEPSUT'S TEMPLE AT DEIR EL BAHARI

Deir el Bahari 147. A last look at part of the surrounding landscape near the temple so much loved and admired.

Deir el Bahari 148. Guards protect an ancient gate that entrances to a nearby structure of the age of the temple.

FREDERICK MONDERSON

Deir el Bahari 149. Final view of the three levels of colonnades and the "Taf-Taf" that now carries visitors to the temple's threshold, for a fee.

Deir el Bahari 150. Some artifacts for sale outside the temple as visitors leave.

HATSHEPSUT'S TEMPLE AT DEIR EL BAHARI

Deir el Bahari 151. More artifacts on display for sale outside the temple as visitors leave.

FREDERICK MONDERSON

Deir el Bahari 152. Merchants offer their wares as Kashida Maloney of Brooklyn (right), another tourist (left) and their guide Hasan Elian (center) leave the temple after an enlightening experience.

27. AFTERWORD

Oftentimes people criticize a work such as this for any number of reasons, primarily because the writer states Hatshepsut was black and that she had a "virgin birth." In the effort to identify the Queen it was stated she was related to Aahmes Nefertari, whose portrait in the British Museum shows a "coal black Ethiopian." As an example, one critic states, no one knows for sure what her color was. That is, 19th Dynasty artisans painted Nefertari's portrait black in praise of her personality. Well, perhaps 19th Dynasty artisans knew more than 19th, 20th and 21st Century critics do. To say that Hatshepsut had a "virgin birth" according to the tale is not surprising. Unquestioned, the ancient Egyptians recognized the creative process is indispensable for childbirth, sex as we understand it. However, for example, the God Min, Amon-Min, is shown with an erect creative tool, but it comes out of his navel not his scrotum, emphasizing the creative process not sex as we know it. When Amon left Karnak for Luxor to cohabitate with Goddess Mut during the Opet Festival, there was no actual sex just the

HATSHEPSUT'S TEMPLE AT DEIR EL BAHARI

philosophic principle of sex between the divinities. Yet, in Hatshepsut's case, the divinity came but that process did not involve sex as we know it. Therefore, it is reasonable to declare Hatshepsut's "Divine birth," given the above.

Deir el Bahari 153. Erik Monderson in Court of Ra-Horakhti's Chapel in 2018.

Deir el Bahari 154. Bird's Eye View of the Upper Portions of the temple.

FREDERICK MONDERSON

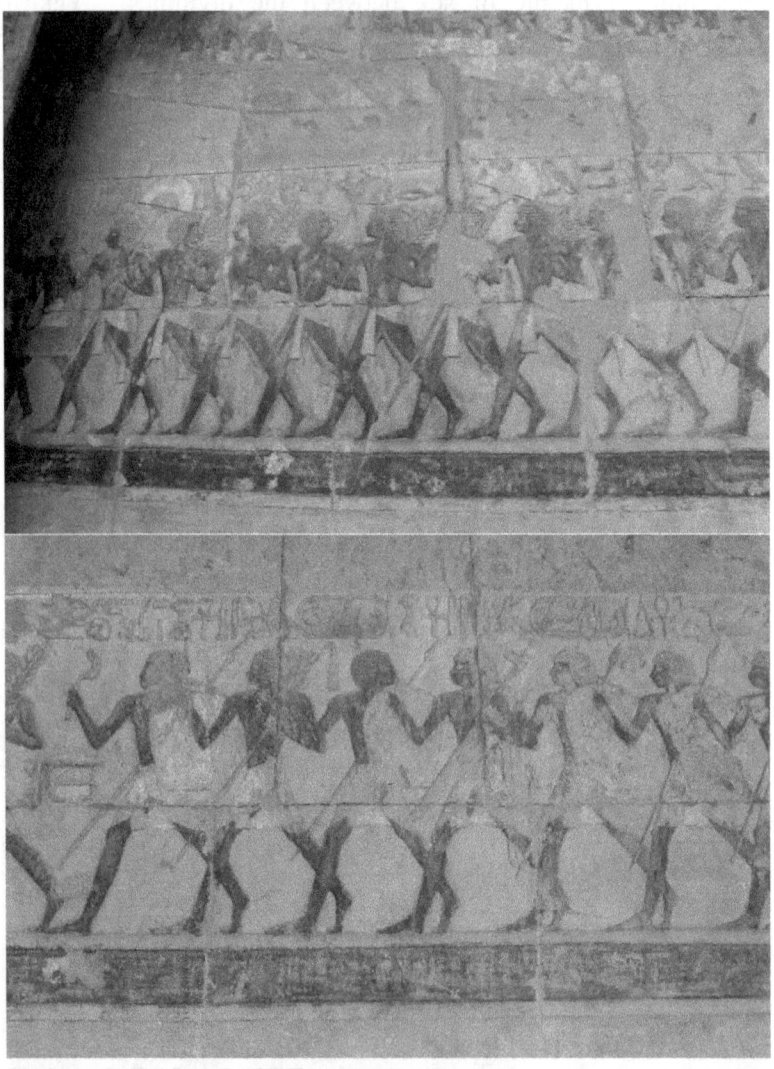

Deir el Bahari 155. "Brothers gonna work it out, Nubian Brothers gonna work it out!"

www.ingramcontent.com/pod-product-compliance
Lightning Source LLC
Chambersburg PA
CBHW071657160426
43195CB00012B/1503